D1546857

DETAIL IN CONTEMPORARY BAR AND RESTAURANT DESIGN

LAURENCE KING

Published in 2013 by
Laurence King Publishing Ltd
361–373 City Road
London
EC1V 1LR
email: enquiries@laurenceking.com
www.laurenceking.com

A catalogue record for this book is
available from the British Library

ISBN: 978 1 78067 060 7

Designed by Olga Reid
Project Editor: Gaynor Sermon
Cover design by Hamish Muir

Printed in China

DETAIL IN CONTEMPORARY BAR AND RESTAURANT DESIGN

**DREW PLUNKETT
AND OLGA REID**

LAURENCE KING PUBLISHING

CONTENTS

3   RESTAURANTS

INTRODUCTION

It is too simple to say that people go to a restaurant because they are hungry or to a bar because they are thirsty. Bars, cafes and restaurants are about something more than eating and drinking. It is obviously more financially prudent to eat at home or picnic in the park but those venues do not quite offer the social dimension that is a crucial component in the rituals of social interaction. People go to meet people they know well, to share the experience of a stimulating environment, and they go to meet people they don't know, using bars and restaurants as a neutral territory better suited to the conduct of business and first social encounters.

A new business will rely on its interior, the first tangible evidence of its intent, to attract its first customers. Initial selection made by the hungriest and thirstiest customers will be as much influenced by the signals given out by its interior as by the food and drink on offer, and the specifics of the design will give explicit information about standards and prices. A good interior can offer some compensation for inadequate products but can not counteract a wholly inadequate experience.

Bar interiors are particularly important in defining the customer experience. The quality of drinks is largely consistent regardless of location and interiors provide the differentiation that can bring success. Degrees of luxury, signalled by quality of materials and detailing, justify variations in price. Expensive materials, extravagant furniture and fittings do not necessarily make for a good interior but, regardless of the components, the quality of detailed execution necessarily requires a level of finessing that demands more time and superior skills.

There are bars, cafes and restaurants that have qualities and continuing success that mean that their interior needs no redesign. They will necessarily require rehabilitation because their fabric, like that of any other interior in the sector, will suffer significant wear and tear, but that should not involve more than the reinstatement of finishes and repairs to furniture. The longer an interior has survived the more antagonistic its habitués and those drawn by its mystique will be to change. Designers aspire to create interiors that will survive, and initial survival will depend on the interior capturing, perhaps defining, the spirit of the time of its creation. Then it must survive the period when it loses its currency until it can assume the status of a period piece, and it is details that will most convincingly express that quality.

Groups, whether gathered for business or pleasure, seek out environments that most effectively accommodate and stimulate their interaction. Individuals will want interaction at one remove, the opportunity to observe other customers in physical and psychological security. But everyone wants what is for them, at the time, the best table and it is not difficult to describe what that is. All aspire to a table against a wall, preferably in a corner and, failing a wall, a column may give adequate anchorage. There is an appeal

about a table having a clearly defined location, a sense of privacy and security offered by an element that belongs, or appears to belong, to the permanent fabric of the original building envelope.

It's accepted wisdom that a long, narrow, rectangular plan will perform most effectively as a bar with the counter running the length of one long wall and banquette seating the length of the other. If the circulation space between is generous enough the bar will be equally effective whether crowded or sparsely populated.

Customers in cafes and restaurants, knowing that they are committed to one table for their stay, tend to have greater concerns about location, and the longer they expect to stay and the greater their anticipated expenditure the more concerned they will be that their table is, at the very least, as good as any other.

When there are no ready made anchoring elements, a strategy that locates bigger tables in the middle of ill-defined space goes some way towards a solution because the bigger the table the more convincingly it assumes the authority of an immovable object. The larger group of customers that populate a table has strength in numbers and, if the table is circular, they create their own self-contained space in which they can ignore the unstructured world that surrounds them.

Tables for one or two are most effectively positioned along the security of existing walls. New partitions strategically planted to subdivide bleak expanses of characterless floor can also provide the elements needed to make desirable locations. Such elements of separation or consolidation may be as high or as low and as solid or as perforated as best suits the project. All offer opportunities for full-blooded detailing.

Detailing may legitimately be about either the creation of blatant spectacle or the definition of something more subtle. The appropriate answer depends on social and cultural context. The utilitarian room that historically fulfilled the demands of bar, cafe and restaurant in one, which grew expediently and organically and required no input from an interior designer, is disappearing as social activities, prompted and sustained by increasing prosperity, take up an increasingly greater proportion of leisure time and become more esoteric. Bars, cafes and restaurants increasingly aim at niche markets as customer groups, determined by age, income, social class and specialist interests seek their own kind in places expressed in design languages that resonate most clearly with them.

Such precision in business plans fine-tunes designers' briefs. The basic elements remain essentially the same, with minor adjustments in dimensions to satisfy the particular ergonomic niceties of eating and drinking that are shaped by gestures towards cultural conventions. The designer's job is not necessarily to compose variations on the well-tried themes of chairs and tables, given the plethora of stylistic options offered by specialist manufacturers and aimed squarely at the hospitality sector, but to orchestrate a harmoniously appropriate whole.

The only furniture elements that are consistently treated as one-off objects are reception desks and bar counters, because they present the first, clearest expression of the interior theme, particular to the business and its location. The practical components and organization are simple, familiar and generally treated prosaically. Cellular arrangements of cupboards and drawers provide the rigid structures that support the defining flourishes which express themes that are also reflected more modestly on walls, floors and ceilings.

The detailing languages that define hospitality interiors were once bluntly expressed in crude stylistic pastiches, especially found in restaurants serving foods particular to one culture. Even in these, the clichés were tuned to the business' location but still sat awkwardly, their credibility undermined by their clumsy artificiality. Perhaps it is the steady spread of many cuisines across both the established and the proliferating prosperous territories of the world that means that the clichés are too familiar to be effective anymore.

The essential ingredients of an international detailing language have evolved with the globalization of leisure and are leading to more subtle and therefore more interesting references and interpretations. There appears to be a diminishing consumer appetite for the pastiches of ethnicity. As holidaymakers travel more widely, they have perhaps become conditioned to seeking bar and restaurant interiors that have some familiarity and are distanced from perceived gastric threats from blatantly local establishments. One might complain that those examples of the new internationalism that take no clues from their produce or their location are themselves becoming a cliché. Ultimately, the outcome of the style war will be decided democratically, by the formulae that succeed, where success is indisputably defined by profit.

As in most interior construction it is the aesthetic rather than the practical priorities that are crucial in generating detail. There are few restraints in the selection of finishes other than that they should have the resilience to deal with persistent erosion by the waves of customers that come with financial success. For cheap outlets, where fast turnover is essential, then the hard and resonating finishes, un-upholstered seats and tables without cloths will encourage short stays and make cleaning easier and faster.

Prices and rents, taxes and services in good locations mean that operating margins are tight and that, with possession of the shell, construction and installation must be carried out quickly so that income generation may begin. This encourages prefabrication off site and collaboration between designer and builder to streamline the means of production. The anticipated life of the chain interior will be comparatively short because the heavy usage associated

with success means that prudently constructed elements will need resuscitation. And crucially, competition will require a fresh representation of visual identity.

Fast turnover and operational efficiency should not mean poor design. Simple construction methods will reduce labour costs in production and installation but the finished interior must attract and retain customers. The standard of design across the chains of fast food restaurants that increasingly dominate city centre streets and shopping malls is high. Such outlets, whether bars, cafes or restaurants have demonstrated the evolutionary truth of the survival of the (aesthetically) fittest and have consistently built customer expectations by presenting increasingly refined interiors, which are frequently more visually sophisticated than the more expensive, and therefore less confrontationally competitive one-off options. They sit between the extremes of the expedient, cash-strapped premises of the small independent operator and the sometimes vulgar extravagances of the expensive alternative.

As the chains, whether cafes, bars or restaurants dominate the mass, but progressively more demanding, markets of the city centres and shopping malls and recognize the need to fine-tune their offer they are increasingly employing their own design managers who are equipped to liaise productively with specialist consultant designers. They invariably choose to compete with interiors that are increasingly sophisticated, that reject the predominantly kitsch ingredients of the early chains with honed and toned aesthetics offering a sophistication not surpassed and frequently surpassing the excesses of more expensive and exclusive rivals that drift towards aesthetic and culinary extremes and eccentricities.

Operators at the upper end of the price spectrum, envisaging a more substantial investment to meet the expectations of a high-end clientele, are generally more inclined to leave matters in the hands of their designers. Details will be executed with extreme refinement and, while the preferences of builders may remain a factor in the evolution of detail, their input, informed by experience of similar projects, is more likely to be productive than restrictive.

An interesting phenomenon, presently confined to western Europe and manifested in modestly scaled and modestly financed one-off establishments is that they rely on found building elements and found objects to provide the palette from which the designer must construct an appropriate detailing language. While distressed finishes and salvaged furniture are becoming a new design cliché, those designers and clients prepared to assemble a palette of economical materials are producing some of the most exciting solutions.

BARS + CAFES

6T7 ESPAI CAFÉ, OLOT
MSB ESTUDI TALLER

The material palette of this cafe responds to the austere grey stone finishes of its immediate surroundings in the Old Town area of Olot in Catalonia. Detailing demonstrates a comparable austerity that positions the new insertions of bar and fixed seating – described by the designers as 'sculptural' in acknowledgement of the bar's secondary role as an exhibition space – at the extreme limits of creature comfort.

The counter, the window seat opposite it and the planes of the long free-standing seating unit are fabricated from steel plates, which were welded on site. Welds were made with great precision so that they do not need to be ground smooth and, like the steel sheets, retain their natural tone and texture. They are strong enough to support the seats which are cantilevered off the backrests. Only the tabletops need a small cantilevered tube support, welded to the vertical centre plates. The steel selected has a dark brown tone and its surface texture has an affinity with the patterns on the rendered walls. Those swirling patterns themselves, made by the plasterer's float on the sand and cement render of the internal walls have a visual affinity with the texture of the stone in the street. The bluer tone of the polished concrete floor screed is complemented by the smooth painted plaster ceiling in which recessed strip lighting follows the lines of the bar counter and fixed seating.

The defining element of the interior, however, is the perforated screen that lines the longer window wall. Its fragility and emphatic texture contrast with the smoother solidity of internal surfaces and furniture pieces but its construction shows the same directness of thinking and making. The screens were constructed in the designers' own workshop. Lengths of steel wire were twisted by hand around welded tubular steel frames, so that each panel is unique. They run continuously along the length of the room and filter light and views to the street. The sun, shining through the panels from midday to the end of the afternoon, casts strong patterns on the steel surfaces and the rear rendered wall. The panels hang from a rail at the junction of ceiling and window and may be slid by hand, to make complex, changing facades.

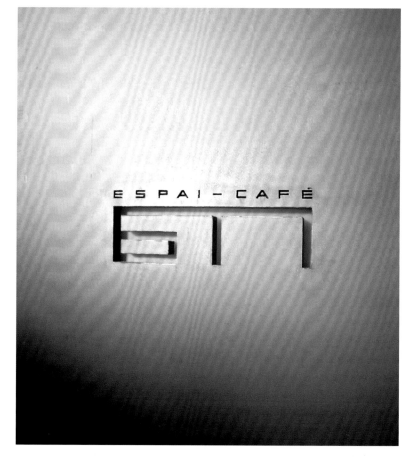

RIGHT, TOP & BOTTOM
The screen stops at the entrance.
The cafe's name is recessed into the
external rendering.

TOP

Textures and tones of wall, floor and ceiling give the interior a solidity that is sympathetic to the traditional buildings of the street beyond the window. Untidy bar equipment is set into recesses formed by new projecting sections of wall.

RIGHT

1 Booth seating
2 Bar counter
3 Window seat
4 Exhibition wall
5 New projecting wall plane
6 Storage recess

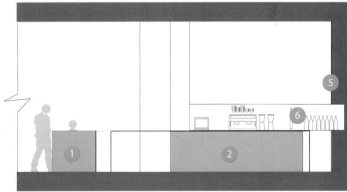

ELEVATION, SCALE 1:100

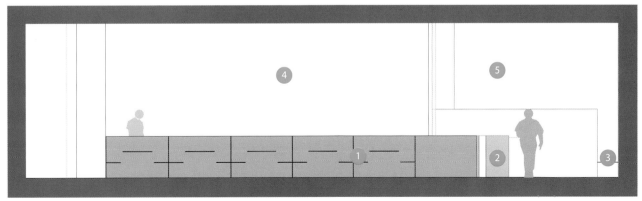

ELEVATION, SCALE 1:100

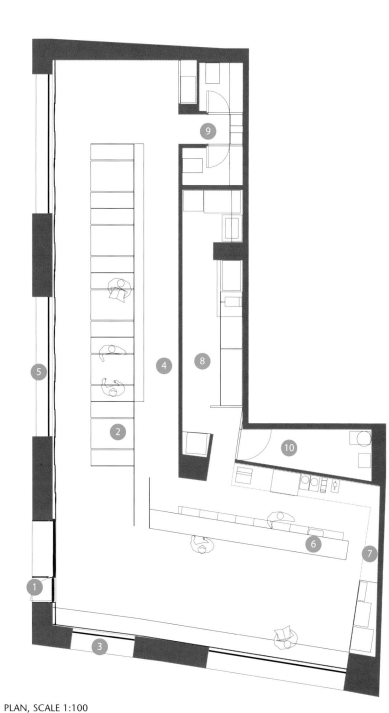

PLAN, SCALE 1:100

TOP

Plan
1 Entrance
2 Booth seating
3 Window seat
4 Exhibition wall
5 Steel wire window screen
6 Bar counter
7 Storage recess
8 Kitchen
9 WCs
10 Storage

TOP RIGHT

Steel wires are stretched continuously between steel tubes to form screen panels. The hand making process produces random patterns.

BOTTOM RIGHT

Screens may be moved to open views to the street.

TOP

Filtered light adds further soft texture to the rendered wall and polished concrete floor. A plate steel counter, with stools, provides additional seating in the exhibition area.

RIGHT

The bar counter and seating booths are fabricated from welded steel plates and form a spine, consolidated by the recessed lights overhead, that unites the two spaces. The booths also define the exhibition area, the entrance to which is marked by two parallel vertical plates, one supporting the top of the bar counter and the other an extension of the side of the booths. Exhibits are hung from a rail at the junction of wall and ceiling.

FEDERAL CAFÉ, BARCELONA
BARBARA APPOLLONI

The cafe occupies a traditional two-storey building with a roof terrace, on a corner site. While the exterior has been left largely unaltered, to remain in keeping with the character of the existing buildings around it, the interior has been radically remodelled to create a strong visual connection between all three levels.

A new concrete stair, cast in situ, with a painted steel balustrade made up of four sheets of 3mm (⅛ in) steel welded together and a 15mm (⅝ in) welded top rail dominates and connects both interior levels, rising through a generous angled void. It is separated by a gap of 100mm (4 in) from the oak-topped, plastered brick balustrade on the first floor. The stair's folded soffits are exposed in both flights and its timber clad, irregularly stepped roof cladding, which doubles as shelving for plants, reminds customers on the terrace of the stair beneath.

The impression of openness is consolidated on the ground floor by steel-framed windows that fold back to connect the interior to the street. The cafe's perimeter is defined by a black tiled wall that, with cushions, doubles as a seat and a table when plywood 'boxes' are hooked over it.

The interior also opens up to a very small internal patio. The table within it is an extension of the cash desk and waiter station that serves both floors and the terrace. Doors on each side of this multi-purpose unit slide open to be concealed within the fixed central panel that exactly matches its width. Waiter stations are clad in plastic laminates on plywood carcasses, as is the preparation and storage bar that slots under the stair, of which the edge profile provides the dominant line that visually resolves the more random placement of shelves and equipment.

On the first floor new wooden framed windows, which match the existing but open outwards to allow another direct link to the exterior, determine the table layout and the triangular void erodes the less desirable area of floor. The oak floor, with wide caulked joints and knots, and the old worn serving table sitting against the void connect the pristine new elements to the traditional architecture of the street.

RIGHT
The ground floor is dominated by two flights of in-situ concrete stairs within the triangular first-floor void.

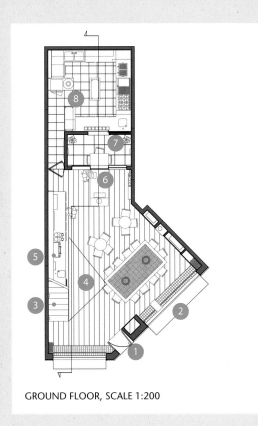

GROUND FLOOR, SCALE 1:200

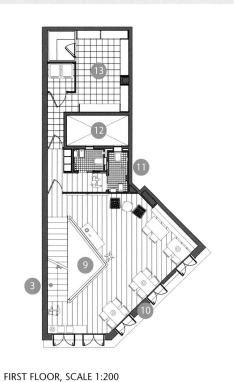

FIRST FLOOR, SCALE 1:200

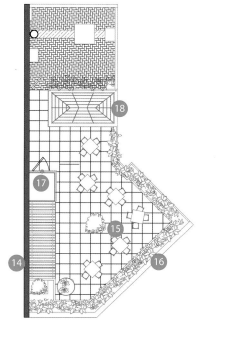

TERRACE, SCALE 1:200

ABOVE

Plans
1 Entrance
2 Window sill/seat/table
3 Stair
4 Void above
5 Preparation and servery below stair
6 Cash desk and waiter station
7 Internal courtyard
8 Kitchen

9 Void
10 New window frames
11 WCs
12 Void over courtyard
13 Storage
14 Stepped planter support
15 External terrace
16 Planter
17 Entrance to stair
18 Glazed roof to courtyard

BELOW

1 Window sill/seat/table
2 Stair
3 Preparation and servery
4 Cash desk and waiter station
5 Table in internal courtyard
6 Services
7 WCs
8 Void over courtyard
9 New window frames

10 Planters
11 Stepped planter support
12 Terrace
13 Entrance to stair
14 Glazed rooflight to courtyard
15 Flat roof

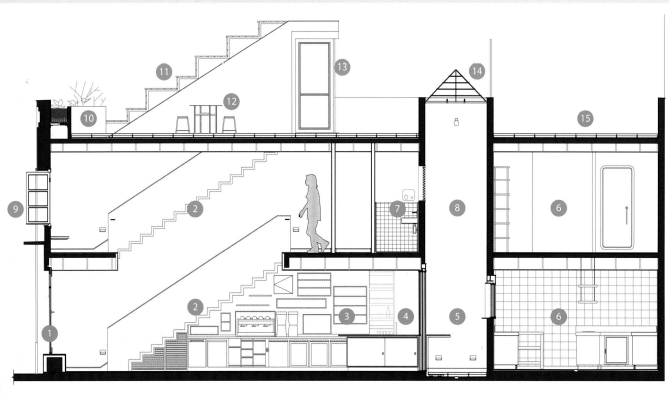

SECTION, SCALE 1:100

ABOVE
The balustrade around the void runs parallel to the external walls. The lampshade on its tripod, coat hanger, base and the painted serving table all relate to the colour of the stair.

RIGHT
First floor: cushions, fixed to fabric with eyelets that slot over steel cylinders on top of the backboard. The laminate on the tabletop and the wall paint relate to the colour of the stairs.

ABOVE LEFT
The tonal variations of the stair's edge, the painted steel balustrade and the painted plaster walls become abstract when framed within the void. The dark metal insert in the oak handrail and screw caps echo the dark grey of the stair.

ABOVE RIGHT
Timber slatted 'steps' on the sloping roof of the stairwell extend the stepped profile of the internal stairs.

LEFT
1 Timber slats
2 Square-section hollow steel tube frame
3 Painted, rendered wall to stair
4 Painted steel window frame
5 Glass
6 Existing facade
7 Planter
8 Tiles

SECTION, SCALE 1:50

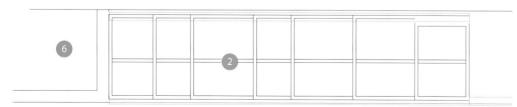

PLAN, SCALE 1:50

ABOVE LEFT
The windows to the street may be folded back so that the black tiled wall can carry cushions for seating and plywood 'tables' whose ends hook over it for stability.

ABOVE RIGHT
The internal courtyard extends views from within the ground floor and provides ventilation.

RIGHT & FAR RIGHT
1 Glazed door
2 Glazed fixed panel
3 Table/counter
4 Existing structure
5 Door closed
6 Counter (inside)
7 Table (courtyard)
8 Door open
9 Steel lintels
10 Fixed panel and doors
11 Tabletop
12 Square-section hollow steel tube bolted to concrete subfloor
13 Paving

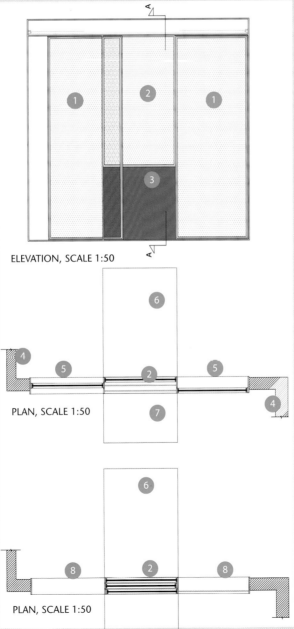

ELEVATION, SCALE 1:50

PLAN, SCALE 1:50

PLAN, SCALE 1:50

SECTION A-A, SCALE 1:25

CORSO,
PARIS
ROBERT STADLER

The intention of this project is to avoid the suggestion of an overriding, and therefore reductive, design concept and to retain some of the informality of the traditional bistro while including new configurations of its traditional elements. The bar, elaborate pendant light fittings and wall mirrors are all reinterpreted so that they have no obvious visual affinity with one another.

The most assertive new element is the coral-pink front of the bar counter, which is assembled from a number of sections, connected by short wedge-shaped, mirror-polished stainless steel junction pieces. The sections are precast in Ductal, a proprietary pre-mixed concrete that allows thinner cross sections to be produced with a high resistance to impact abrasion and chemical erosion. The circular tabletops and legs are cast in grey Ductal, which relates to the colour of the walls. Occasional pink versions carry the counter colour into the body of the room. Neither version makes an obvious concession to the more traditional wooden chairs.

The inverted dish light fittings are conventional in form but their size and number suggest another departure from the familiar. Their reflective inside surface is gilded with gold adhesive tape, the ends of which are cut square but short of the bottom of the shade to make a ragged edge, which implies a relaxed aesthetic that avoids an overbearing stylistic rigour. Wall-mounted lights share the ragged ends and double as menu blackboards.

Stepped mirror edges break up the flat planes of internal walls. The rectangular mirror panels are fixed flush with the wall surface and the stepped pattern is applied with the same paint as is used for the plaster finish, which overcomes the difficulty of matching profiles of wall and mirror. The irregular mirror shapes fragment and disrupt views of the reflected images of the interior, to more effectively suggest a different space beyond the opaque surfaces. Isolated shelves for bottles behind the bar and books in the public area conform to the principle of ostensibly random horizontals.

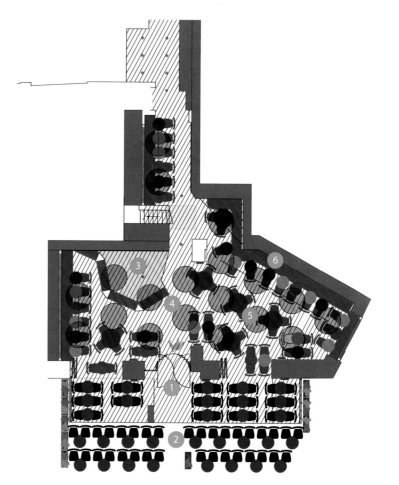

PLAN, SCALE 1:200

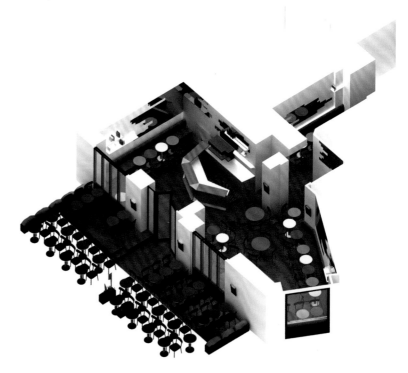

OPPOSITE
The room is dominated by the gilded pendant lights and pink bar front.

TOP RIGHT
Plan
1 Entrance
2 Terrace
3 Bar
4 Light fitting
5 Table and chairs
6 Perimeter seating

BOTTOM RIGHT
Axonometric

ABOVE
Applying the adhesive gold tape. The ends are protected by masking tape during the process.

LEFT
The reflective tape hugely dramatizes the effect of the single light bulb.

ELEVATION, SCALE 1:25

ABOVE
Matt yellow wall bites into the rectangle suggested by the mirror, shown in grey.

BOTTOM LEFT
The wall light and menu board has the same ragged edge as the mirror and light fitting. The windows reflected in the mirror open onto the street terrace.

BOTTOM RIGHT
Ragged-edged mirrors break up the wall planes and suggest other rooms beyond. Bookshelves continue the horizontal emphasis.

TOP LEFT
The moulds for the counter front and table base.

MIDDLE LEFT
Pouring the liquid Ductal into the base mould.

BOTTOM LEFT
Section and plan drawings of table.

BOTTOM RIGHT
Some tables are coloured pink to match the counter front and some grey to match the walls.

OPPOSITE TOP
Elevation of the bar counter. Segments of mirror, shown grey, are set into corners.

OPPOSITE BOTTOM LEFT
The front will shield the conventional bar storage and worktop.

OPPOSITE BOTTOM RIGHT
A reflective 55 degree brass wedge piece connects the lengths of bar counter front.

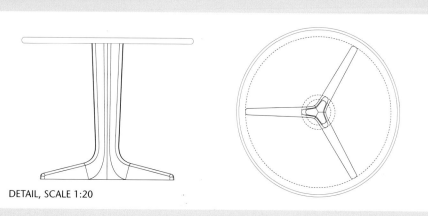

DETAIL, SCALE 1:20

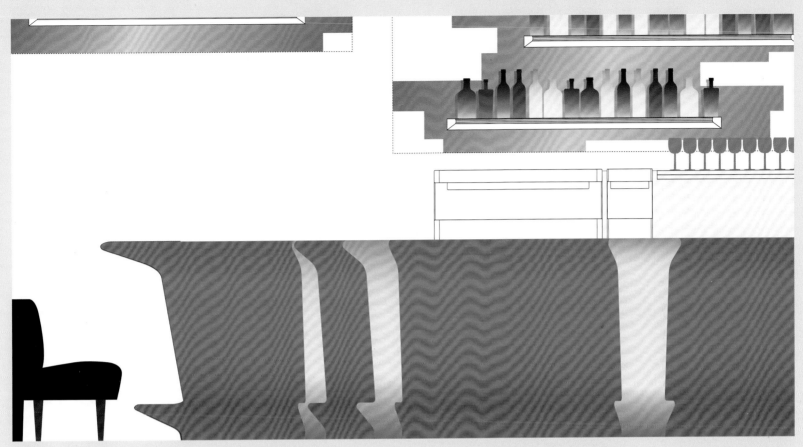

SECTION, SCALE 1:20

CONFISERIE BACHMANN, BASEL
HHF

This renovation of a flagship coffee house and chocolate shop for Confiserie Bachmann, a manufacturer with a reputation for high quality confectionery, sets out to express the traditional values of the brand through a more contemporary interpretation of the business' existing interior.

A covered passageway that runs through the existing building is accessed by glazed doors and makes a protected place for outdoor seating. Light colours and highly reflective surfaces increase the brightness of the room. The simple off-white geometry of the entrance lobby that provides a transition between the traditional stone doorway of the original building and the restraint of the new, feeds customers directly to the retail counter, which occupies the greater proportion of the floor area in the triangle created by the cafe zone along the wall to the passageway.

Generous circulation space around the counters and window display cabinets make an efficient retail provision and left over space within the retail triangle is devoted to communal tables that are integral to the display and service counters. The significant mass of the counter units is broken up by the articulation of functional elements within them and further dematerialized by reflections in their stainless steel vertical and horizontal surfaces. A wall of top-lit, offset mirrors that wraps around two sides of the triangle increases the perceived size and complexity of the room.

Large round-cornered pendant lights hang over and help define the cafe area and their white cuboid shades provide a counterpoint to the dark round tables, their mirrored soffits add to the visual complexity. The conventional dark brown tables, chairs and stools make the only overt reference to chocolate.

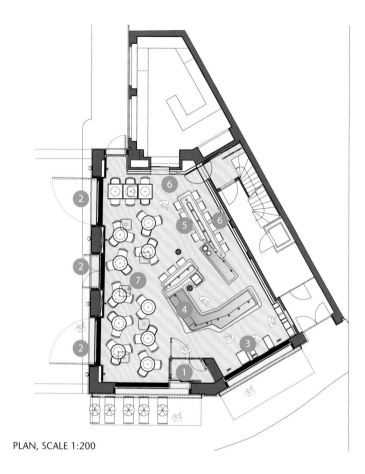

PLAN, SCALE 1:200

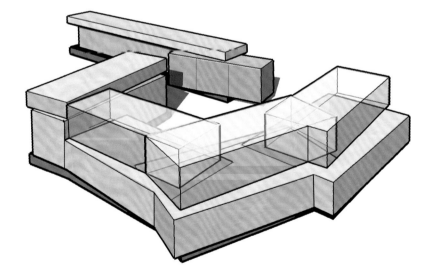

TOP
Plan
1 New entrance lobby
2 New doors to covered outdoor area
3 Window display
4 Counter and display
5 Communal table
6 Mirrored walls
7 Pendant light fittings

RIGHT
Articulation of functional elements within the counters breaks up their bulk.

OPPOSITE TOP
The high reflectivity of the counter tops and front reduces their mass and the mirrored underside of the cuboid light fittings further deconstructs planes.

OPPOSITE BOTTOM LEFT
The street and ceiling are reflected in the communal tabletop. The mirrored wall behind erodes the perimeter.

OPPOSITE BOTTOM RIGHT
The cafe area looking towards the entrance lobby. Bar stools match the chairs and tables.

DAS NEUE KUBITSCHECK, MUNICH
DESIGNLIGA

This cafe is owned by a German environmentalist punk (mission statement: 'Fuck the cake mix') who aims to preserve the best of the German confectionery tradition but aspires to present it in a context that suggests neither respectability nor connoisseurship. To achieve this he commissioned a multidisciplinary design team who could produce both an interior with a suitably provocative ambience and the printed ephemera to expand and promote his philosophy.

Apart from the cuboids that cascade from one corner behind the counter, three of which display examples of the 'new confectionery', the rest of the interior utilizes familiar and utilitarian elements although they are brought together with a degree of discord. It offers minimal creature comforts, as if to concentrate hedonistic impulses on cake consumption.

Detailing is direct and simple. The counter front is tongue-and-groove boarding, perversely vertical in what is a predominantly horizontal unit and it supports a mundane but efficient display cabinet. The wall brackets that support the shelves are substantial, with a visual affinity for the bent steel legs of the long wooden benches that structure the furniture layout but promise little physical comfort. Considered diversity of detailing becomes the unifying element. The white bench relates to the white counter and the unpainted bench to the skirting that runs beneath all blocks of wall colour.

While the objects and elements are simple and broadly familiar, the incongruous juxtapositions, like the Eames DSR chairs with their plastic shells and spindly metal legs sitting on the intricately traditionally patterned rug, set up provocative interactions. Pendant lights hang in undisciplined configurations but other delicate, considered details, like the glass-covered chessboard recessed into a tabletop, signal that everything has been deliberately and precisely thought through.

TOP
The chessboard set into the table connects to tradition. The printed material points to the future.

BOTTOM LEFT
Pink chairs, tables and mission statement superimposed on the conventional name and generic description, signal changes in the world of the traditional cafe.

BOTTOM RIGHT
The pink jacket complements the grey and ensures the exterior colour appears on the back wall.

OPPOSITE TOP
Boxes cascading from the wall suggest that the superficially ordinary elements of counter, display cabinet and shelves deserve consideration.

OPPOSITE BOTTOM LEFT
Axonometric.

OPPOSITE BOTTOM RIGHT
Austere wooden benches structure the plan. Other elements act as, apparently random, focal points.

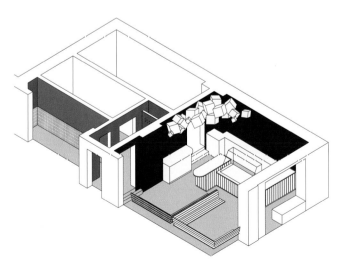

CAFÉ FOAM,
STOCKHOLM
NOTE DESIGN STUDIO

When a client asks for an interior that people will love or hate and to which no one can be indifferent, designers are faced with the problem of provoking a range of extreme and conflicting emotions without being able to cater to a single clear customer profile. Note Design Studio turned to bull-fighting, its tensions, its movements and its colours to initiate their creative process, setting perceived Spanish emotion against presumed Scandinavian restraint.

There are three areas within the interior, a 'Scandinavian' restaurant at one end and a 'Spanish' lounge at the other. Colours and materials from lounge and restaurant come together in the third, the entrance and bar area. 'Spanish' territory is defined by areas of strong pinkish red against textured ochre walls. Its entrance is marked by a pinkish-red screen with angled internal framing. Beyond that the room is more enclosed than the others, curtains hung from ceiling-mounted rails drop to the floor to separate areas for individual tables. The chairs, here with black frames and charcoal grey upholstery are otherwise the same as those in the restaurant, where frames are natural Scandinavian wood and the upholstery is light grey. Plywood predominates in the Scandinavian zone, where it is used for the floor, walls and ceiling and meets abutting finishes in angled slashes.

Scandinavian and Spanish influences come together in the entrance/bar with colours and materials interlocking. The two-dimensional angle, at which the plywood cladding that forms the backdrop to the bar in the entrance area meets the raw plaster, sets up the three-dimensional angles of the bar front. Other fragments of plywood line door openings and recessed shelving.

The coloured glass light fittings were especially designed and made for this project; there is a preponderance of red in the restaurant and a more natural green in the lounge, as if the two have swapped. The entrance mixes a few of each colour with its own white and clear versions.

TOP
A view from the entrance to the 'Scandinavian' room: raw plaster makes an angled junction with plywood cladding and generates the profile of the bar front.

MIDDLE
The angled screen marks the entrance to the more enclosed 'Spanish' room.

BOTTOM
Red walls and curtains against the ochre wall are inspired by perceptions of Spain. Dark chairs contrast with the lighter models in the 'Scandinavian' room but the green glass light fittings suggest the Northern palette.

TOP
The 'Spanish' red spills into the entrance space, painted on the otherwise raw grey plaster.

BOTTOM LEFT
1 Entrance
2 Arrival bar
3 'Spanish' room
4 'Scandinavian' room
5 Bar servery

BOTTOM RIGHT
Light coloured plywood on floor, walls and ceiling, light coloured furniture and the blue/grey walls define 'Scandinavian' territory. The colours of the cushions, light fittings and the pink/red corridor are borrowed from the 'Spanish' palette.

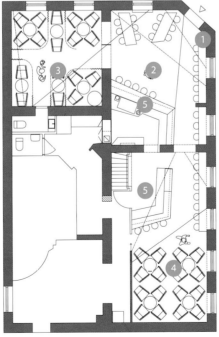

PLAN, SCALE 1:200

MOCHA MOJO,
CHENNAI
MANCINI ENTERPRISES

At first glance the construction principle behind this intense interior appears to follow the familiar logic of stacked children's building blocks, which makes for an accessible aesthetic.

Necessarily functional elements, such as the stairs and shop counter, are concealed behind or within seemingly random assemblies of rectilinear three-dimensional strips that bear little obvious relationship to the practical form of the elements they front. The apparently arbitrary deployment of paint colours further deconstructs familiar interior elements.

Construction was inevitably more complicated than its visual affinity with interlocking bricks might suggest. The designers found that the most effective way of conveying their intentions to the builders was to rationalize the three-dimensional matrix and divide the two storeys of the original shell into 25 layers, each conforming to one of three standard depths. Each horizontal strip was subdivided into random lengths and a colour specified for each component. They claim that carpenters and painters had fun interpreting the diagrams setting out these instructions. All elements were cut and assembled on site from MDF sheet and finished, after installation, with primer, filler and two coats of acrylic emulsion paint.

The designer/communication technique was effective, not only for describing the composition of wall claddings, but also for explaining the configuration of freestanding elements, like the floor-mounted sales and cashier's counters and chandelier and small seating booth that are suspended in the void. The depths of the striations on these freestanding pieces match those of the wall claddings at an equivalent height above base level.

The three-dimensional strips adapted easily to conceal the light sources that wash across the vertical or horizontal faces of adjacent units as well as cabling, coolant piping and condensation drains. The white gloss finish of the tables, plastic chairs and stools share the surface reflectivity of the boxes and upholstered pads match their tonal values. The self-levelling resin floor provides another highly reflective, strongly-coloured plane. The loose canvas cushions, also colour matched to the box colours, are the only soft elements.

MEZZANINE PLAN, SCALE 1:200

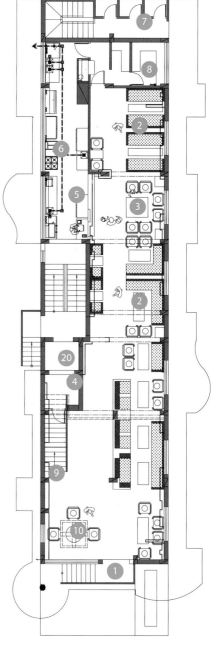

GROUND FLOOR PLAN, SCALE 1:200

ABOVE
Plan
1 Entrance
2 Fixed seating integrated with bands
3 Loose seating
4 Merchandize counter integrated with bands
5 Cashier
6 Kitchen
7 Storage
8 Staff
9 Stair to mezzanine integrated with bands
10 Chandelier
11 Void
12 Suspended two-person booth

13 Bridge
14 Handrail integrated with bands
15 Service integrated with bands
16 Hookah station
17 Projection screen
18 Male WC
19 Female WC
20 Lift

OPPOSITE
A view across the bridge to the suspended booth, the existing 'boxed' column and the lower level. The chandelier hangs on the right, its horizontally graded colours matching those of the column and the walls.

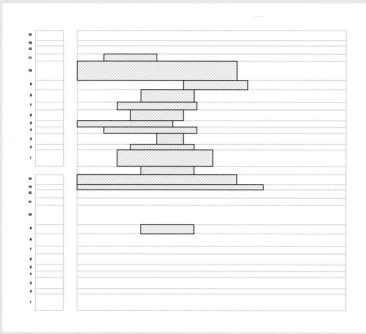

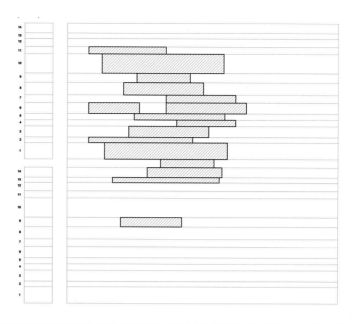

ABOVE
The horizontal bars of the chandelier, suspended in the void, match the depth of the wall bands at the same height above floor level.

LEFT
Loose furniture matches the precision of form and surface reflectivity of the wall boxes.

OPPOSITE TOP
A view from the suspended booth across the bridge to the mezzanine and down through the void.

OPPOSITE BOTTOM
1 Existing structural column
2 Edge of mezzanine
3 Existing overhead structural beam
4 Steel bridge structure
5 Suspension cable
6 Steel suspended frame
7 Existing roof slab
8 Seat
9 Table

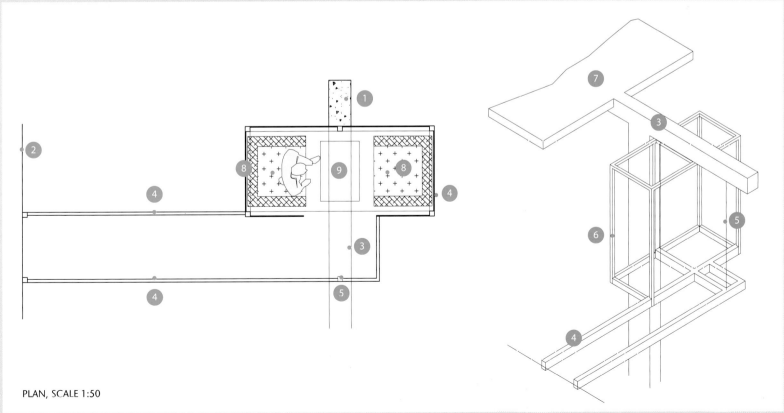

PLAN, SCALE 1:50

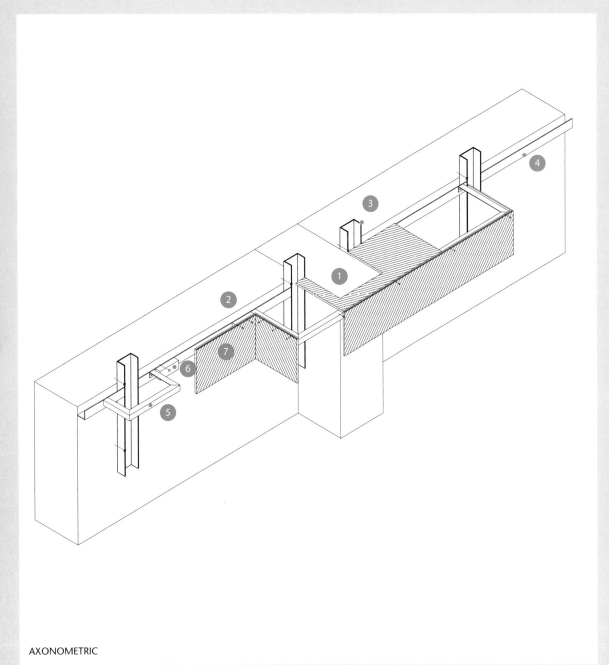

AXONOMETRIC

LEFT & BOTTOM
1 Existing column
2 Existing wall
3 Steel channel fixed to wall
4 40 x 40mm (1½ x 1½ in) 'L' angle welded to channel
5 25 x 25mm (1 x 1 in) 'L' angle welded to 40 x 40mm (1½ x 1½ in) 'L' angle
6 100 x 40 x 25mm (4 x 1½ x 1 in) timber spacer
7 9mm (⅜ in) Gypsum or MDF board screwed to frame

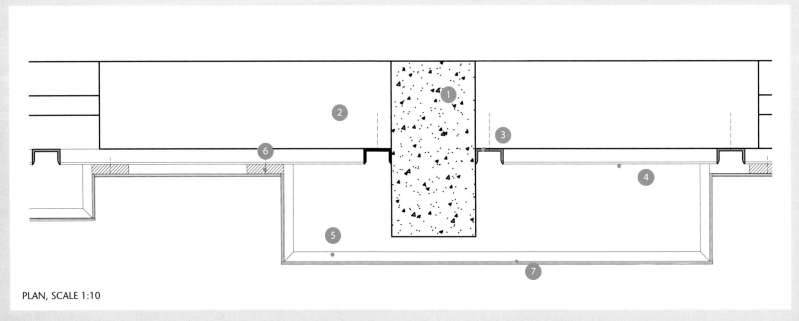

PLAN, SCALE 1:10

ABOVE
The cladding to practical elements, such as the handrail to the stair and the sales counter, match the depth and colour of wall bands at equivalent heights.

RIGHT
Boxes conceal light sources that wash up and down wall surfaces. Canvas cushions provide the only visually 'soft' elements.

SALON DES SALUTS, TOKYO
SINATO

In this small wine bar the boundary between the interior and the street is made ambiguous by the insertion of four glass boxes that project in front of and behind the line of the facade of the upper building. The demarcation is further blurred by a zone of plants on the street boundary that grow both inside and outside the boxes.

Each box has its own function. One, open to the street with a glass door on its inner face, acts as an entrance vestibule, approached on isolated steps, set between plants that match the floor tiles of the interior. A second, with a table and two chairs and without a roof, is described as a 'terrace', isolated from the main bar area by the glass door that forms one of its shorter sides. This roofless space acts as a smoking area and the steel-trimmed circle cut in one glass wall supplies fresh air. The largest, with a table and bench seating that may be reserved, is open to the main bar and has a 'roof' of horizontal sheet glass. The smallest box holds an olive tree.

Each box consists of glass quadrant corner sections and varying straight lengths, one of which also acts as a door in three of the units. Joints in the glass are sealed with clear silicon and secured top and bottom by stainless steel frames, which are in turn fixed for stability to structural elements below the finished floor and above the suspended ceiling. In three of the boxes the glass and frame sections are cantilevered beyond the tiled internal floor to allow planting to cross into what is perceived as interior space. The square floor tiles of the interior are cut to make a serpentine line where they meet the planting. Spaces between boxes are closed with acrylic panels set in silicon.

The lowered ceiling immediately inside the line of the existing building, which contains air-conditioning equipment and hides the high-level fixings for the glass sections, is clad in cedar boarding, as are the structures built around the existing column, which contains the waiter service station and storage, and the lavatory that mark its inner limit. Other walls and ceiling areas are plastered and painted. An illuminated pink strip recessed into two of the plastered walls wraps around the seating area.

RIGHT
The new facade of four boxes projects beyond the brick facade of the original multistorey building. The box on the left contains the olive tree. The next is the reservation space which is 'roofed' with a glass sheet where it projects beyond the original facade line. The third is the entrance with tile steps up from street level. The last is the 'terrace', open to the sky. The concrete perimeter strip raises planting to inner floor level.

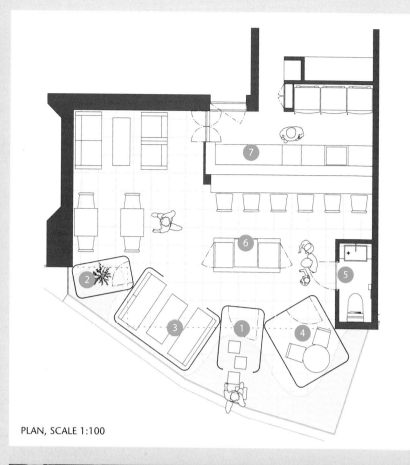

PLAN, SCALE 1:100

LEFT
Plan
1 Entrance
2 Court
3 Private room
4 Terrace
5 WC
6 Storage
7 Counter

BOTTOM
The glass is clamped between stainless steel strips fixed above and below floor and ceiling. That of the inner walls pivots to become doors at the entrance and to the 'terrace' and olive 'court'. Where tiling meets planting it is cut to make a serpentine junction.

OPPOSITE TOP LEFT
Rain water is drained from the open 'terrace'.

OPPOSITE TOP RIGHT
Cantilevering of frame and glass allow planting to pass through the new facade. The circular opening provides additional ventilation in this unroofed 'terrace'.

OPPOSITE BOTTOM
Detailed plans
1 Entrance
2 Court
3 Private room
4 Terrace
5 WC
6 Stainless steel frame
7 Glass
8 Acrylic filler piece
9 Stainless steel U-channel end piece

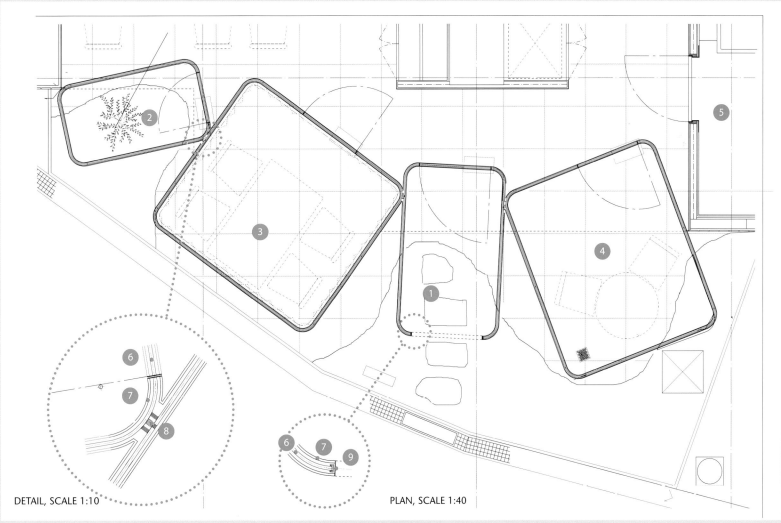

DETAIL, SCALE 1:10

PLAN, SCALE 1:40

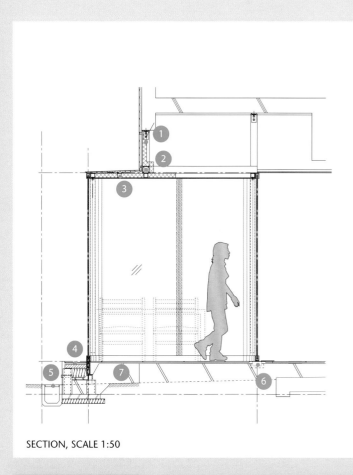

SECTION, SCALE 1:50

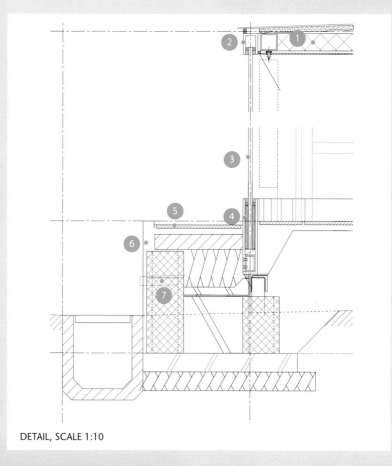

DETAIL, SCALE 1:10

TOP LEFT
Private room: section
1 45mm (1¾ in) insulation
2 Square hollow-section steel bolted to existing structure
3 Square hollow-section steel connecting upper glass framing
4 Porcelain tiles
5 Existing gutter
6 New concrete floor section
7 Floor hinge

TOP RIGHT
Private room: section details
1 Stainless steel sheets on anti-condensation insulation
2 6mm (⅜ in) stainless steel window frame
3 Two sheets toughened glass with anti-shatter film core
4 6mm (⅜ in) stainless steel frame supporting glass
5 Porcelain tile on mortar bed on concrete screed
6 Trowelled mortar upstand
7 Drainage hole

BOTTOM
Within the monochromatic and hard-edged interior timber, cloth upholstery, translucent glass tabletops and woven seating make textural connections to the planting.

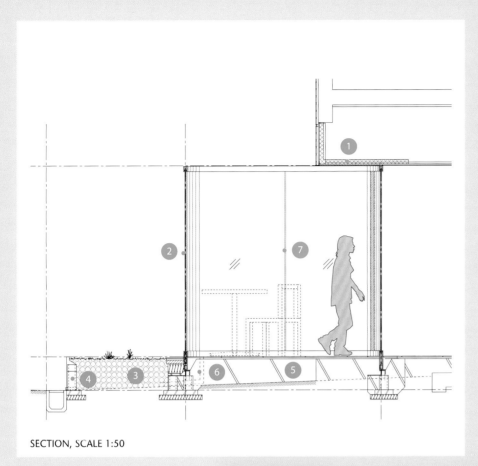

SECTION, SCALE 1:50

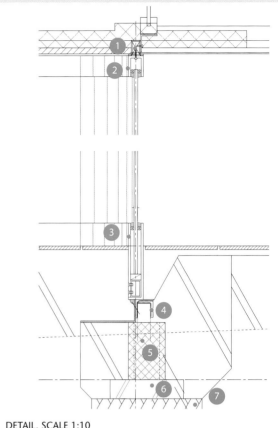

DETAIL, SCALE 1:10

TOP LEFT

Terrace: section
1 Veneered plywood as interior with clear urethane waterproofing
2 Glass wall supported on proprietary stainless steel glazing system
3 Planting box
4 Trowelled mortar upstand
5 Concrete levelling fill
6 Connection to drainage
7 Silicon joint

TOP RIGHT

Terrace: section details
1 Sealant
2 6mm (⅜ in) stainless steel frame: upper edge
3 6mm (⅜ in) stainless steel frame: lower edge
4 Welded steel substructure
5 Masonry
6 Concrete levelling fill
7 Hardcore

BOTTOM

Cedar boards clad the lowered ceiling and service blocks. The illuminated pink strip wraps round the inner seating area.

Z AM PARK, ZURICH
AEKAE

As befits a cafe in a park this interior makes no fussy or flamboyant gestures. Its identity is more quietly established by what may, at first, appear to be an ad hoc collection of reclaimed or recycled elements; these make an interior that is modest enough to relate to its location in a former workers' district of the city and robust enough to co-exist with the views, through the large windows and across its terrace, of trees in the park. However, on closer examination, each element turns out to have an idiosyncrasy that amplifies its understated installation and intervention.

If there is a single dominant element it is probably the oak herringbone parquet flooring, recycled from the cafe's previous manifestation and now glued to a plywood carcass and redeployed as a finishing veneer for the bar counter and perimeter bench seating. It shows enough evidence of wear to point to its previous existence, hidden under layers of carpet and linoleum, as the floor of the original 1950s cafe. Its rough textures contrast with the smooth poured concrete floor finish that replaces it.

The hard-edged geometry of the fixed seating, perhaps more likely to be found in exterior furniture, is made comfortable with loose foam cushions and backrests, which are covered in recycled curtain material that introduces patina, pattern and informality. This is underpinned by the customization, by five invited designers and artists, of four of the classic Horgenglarus bistro chairs. These variations are used for six months before being auctioned and replaced by more reworked chairs, with the profit going to the participating designers. This 'Take a Seat' project was started as part of the interior concept of Z am Park.

Modular light fittings, designed in 1965, crowd the ceilings, suggesting the branches of the trees in the park, and contrast with the variously styled brass candlesticks that are distributed casually throughout the space and represent those artefacts likely to be found in a traditional cafe. A more decorative tradition is also acknowledged in the low-level frieze strip, laser cut from brass coloured film and mounted on the outside of the windows, and in the design of the menu.

PLAN, SCALE 1:100

TOP
Plan
1 Entrance
2 Terrace
3 Fixed seating
4 Bar
5 Kitchen
6 WCs

MIDDLE
The worn joints of the parquet veneer contrast with the delicacies of patterned fabrics and candlesticks. Brass edge lipping upgrades the laminate-covered table and is echoed in the window frieze.

BOTTOM
The herringbone pattern of the parquet is complemented by the angled and chamfered counter front.

TOP
Large windows make the park an important element within the interior. The recycling of the parquet flooring as fixed seating and curtain fabric as cushion covers bring patina and pattern, which are counterpointed by the smooth grey walls and floor. The black fabric backrest customizes an archetypical cafe chair.

BOTTOM LEFT
A laser-cut brass motif is glued to the inside of the windows.

BOTTOM RIGHT
Dense clusters of ceiling lights suggest the branches of trees in the park and contrast sharply with traditional candlesticks.

VINEGAR CAFE, FUKUOKA
HIMEMATSU ARCHITECTURE

The cafe is set within the shell of a 130-year-old private house and serves dishes based on the varieties of vinegar produced in the small factory attached to it. The original exterior of the house is preserved to harmonize with its location within a quiet village and the surrounding countryside. The interior of the cafe is less compromising. Rough-hewn beams are the only evidence of the existing structure. Tables and chairs are conceived as aggregated extrusions of the 105mm (4⅛ in) wide boards on the floor, walls and ceiling, which suggest timber bands that run continuously around the room.

This may be seen as a typical example of uncompromising Japanese design where the utilitarian is sacrificed for the conceptual and, as such, sits comfortably within a culture that respects ritual and ideas above comfort and convenience. The furniture may also be seen as an allusion to the stones placed precisely on the raked sand, which is here represented here by the lines of the floorboards, in a traditional garden. Since views to the gardens through the windows on both ends of the room are crucial to the experience of the interior, the furniture, without any hint of kitsch, makes an appropriate bridge between the two.

Both tables and chairs are made with thin layers of bendable plywood, stiffened by thicker plywood ribs. They are painted with the floor paint for consistency of finish and durability, and fixed in position so that the precision of the layout may not be disturbed. The display shelves repeat the same construction technique but, like the posts and beams, are painted a lighter blue to distinguish them from the bands that encircle the room.

TOP RIGHT
The exterior of the original private house.

MIDDLE RIGHT
Display shelves continue the principle of extruded bands but are painted in a lighter tone to indicate their secondary status.

BOTTOM RIGHT
1 Entrance
2 Cafe
3 Kitchen
4 Factory
5 Shop counter
6 WC

OPPOSITE PAGE
All elements that are defined by the 105mm (4⅛ in) board width are painted darker blue. The original beams, timber posts and shelving are a lighter tone.

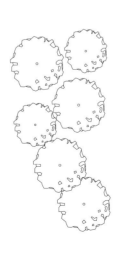

PLAN, SCALE 1:100

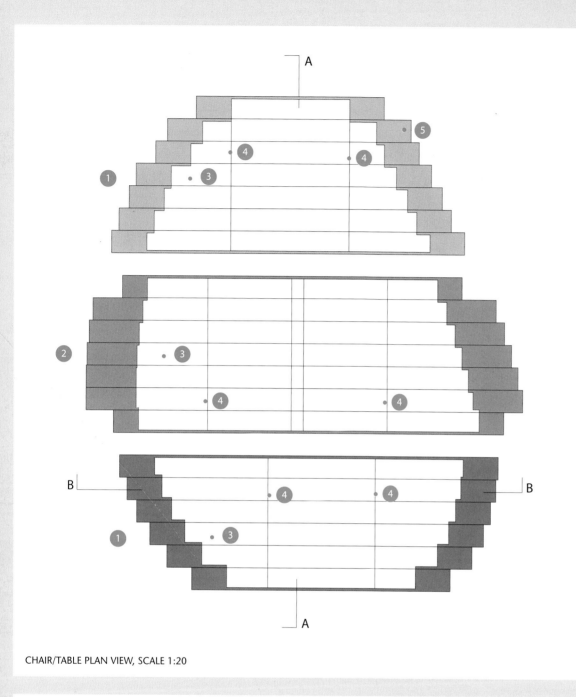

LEFT
Plan view of table and seating
1 Seating
2 Table
3 Cross rib
4 Lateral rib
5 Painted external skin

BOTTOM LEFT
Section through seating
1 Cross ribs
2 Lateral ribs
3 Painted external skin

CHAIR/TABLE PLAN VIEW, SCALE 1:20

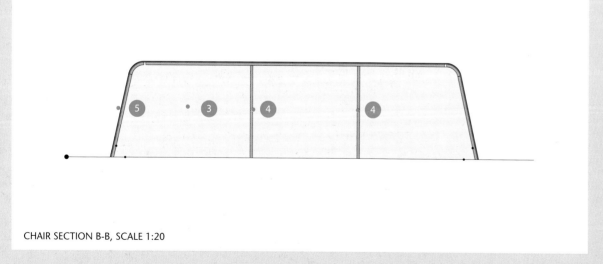

CHAIR SECTION B-B, SCALE 1:20

RIGHT
Section through seating and table units
1 Table
2 Seating
3 Cross rib
4 Lateral rib
5 Painted external skin

BOTTOM
Tables and seating together suggest one unit, resembling the stones that sit in isolation in the garden. The bands in the tables and bench line precisely with the wall and floor boarding.

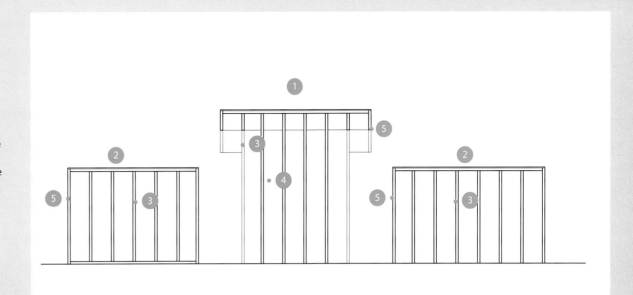

SECTION A-A, SCALE 1:20

AG CAFE, NAGOYA
KIDOSAKI ARCHITECTS STUDIO

The owner of this cafe wanted to sell art. He wanted a changing display of pictures and sculptures to give his cafe its character but understood that an interior wholly committed to the preferential display of artefacts was not necessarily going to attract customers who were looking for a cafe. Therefore it was in the interests of both sides of the business to find a solution that would attract customers principally interested in one or other offering and who might, perhaps, be encouraged to make a crossover purchase.

The designers accepted that their contribution had to remain restrained and that the artefacts displayed would and should provide the dominant visual interest, but they also recognized that modest gestures were necessary to establish the cafe component's independent identity. For practical reasons they chose to construct a new wall directly in front of the projecting structural piers on the longest wall, to provide an uninterrupted and flexible display area. They then used the void created behind the new wall to conceal back lighting for a continuous and complex pattern cut into the wall panels where they met the ceiling. The illuminated strip becomes an equivalent of the cornice mouldings that masked the junction between wall and ceiling plaster in traditional construction. The pattern is complemented by Ronan and Erwan Bouroullec's Vegetal chairs.

The perforated strip was produced using CNC technology, an automated making process that links CAD, or computer aided design, directly to CAM, or computer aided manufacturing. Its speed and precision makes possible the production of elements that would not be economically viable if carried out by hand. The delicate complexity of the 'bird's nest' motif required a 5mm radius router, the smallest CNC cutting tool available and the intricacy of the pattern required a slightly longer production time but this increase, was negligible when compared to that necessary had hand making techniques been employed.

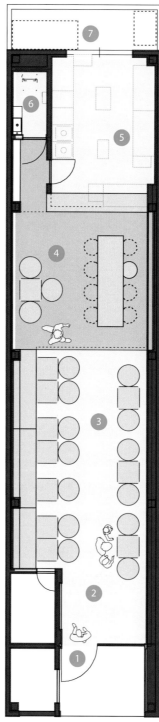

PLAN, SCALE 1:100

ABOVE
1 Entrance
2 Exhibition wall
3 Lower cafe
4 Upper cafe
5 Kitchen
6 WC
7 Store

OPPOSITE TOP RIGHT
The walls to the kitchen and opposite the exhibition are heavily modelled.

OPPOSITE FAR RIGHT
The new wall runs the length of the cafe and links both levels.

BOTTOM RIGHT
CNC allows complex, non-repeating patterns to be drawn and cut quickly and economically.

BOTTOM FAR RIGHT
The exhibition wall, topped by the 'bird's nest' frieze, sits in front of existing columns, which are just visible above it, to make an uninterrupted display surface. Backlighting maximizes the impact of the pattern.

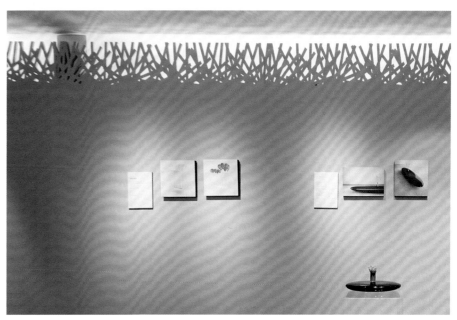

ZMIANATEMATU, LODZ
XM3

Lodz is the third largest city in Poland and is committed to establishing itself as the centre for the country's design, fashion and film industries, whose practitioners are expected to form the nucleus of customers for this cafe, which is housed on the ground floor of a neoclassical building on the city's major thoroughfare. Since the nineteenth century the interior had been serially adapted for various diverse activities and nothing original remained of any significance. The designers, prompted by a tight budget, were, however, happy to retain existing rough and mundane finishes as modest backdrops for the new defining element, a service counter that transmutes into ceiling and seating. The 15mm (⅝ in) thick raw plywood used in its construction has an affinity with the sections of existing wall, as does the black surface-mounted conduit that carries new electric wiring. New walls and those adjacent to the refurbished external facade are painted white. Those on the new walls to the toilet area are embellished with murals with imagery that suggests graffiti and implies a decadent recent phase in the life of the building.

The ribbed structure was first explored digitally as a solid and, when definitively established, translated, again by computer, into a series of ribs, at regular centres. Individual rib components were fabricated off site using CNC machinery. Time spent generating digital data for each progressive variation being inconsequential when compared to that required to mark out and cut one-off pieces by hand.

Where individual ribs were too big to be cut from one sheet of plywood, CNC precision made possible the production of interlocking 'jigsaw' devices, cut into abutting end pieces, which gave not only rigid connections and exact alignments but also a decorative motif to punctuate the length. The metal brackets that fix ribs in position are plainly visible and their utilitarian directness matches that of the plywood and the electrical conduit. When exploring and testing CNC techniques the designers produced a number of complex three-dimensional forms, in 12mm (½ in) plywood, that were then adapted to form the base structure of low, glass-topped tables.

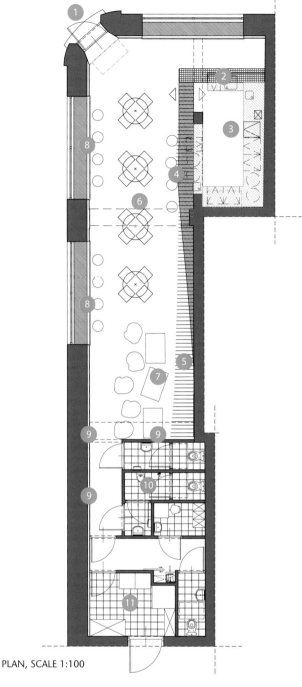

PLAN, SCALE 1:100

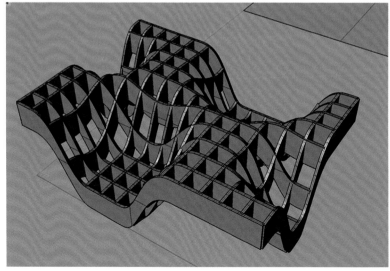

TOP
1 Entrance
2 Bar counter
3 Kitchen
4 Plywood bar counter on rib supports
5 Seating on rib supports
6 Ceiling ribs
7 CNC tables
8 Window 'shelf' table
9 Mural
10 WCs
11 Office

BOTTOM
Experiments with CNC techniques became bases for glass-topped tables.

TOP
Ribs mask an existing column and sweep up to form the ceiling and down to make shelving behind the bar. The menu written on the ribs is appropriately casual.

BOTTOM
Ribs adapt easily to make display shelves. Horizontal pieces brace verticals.

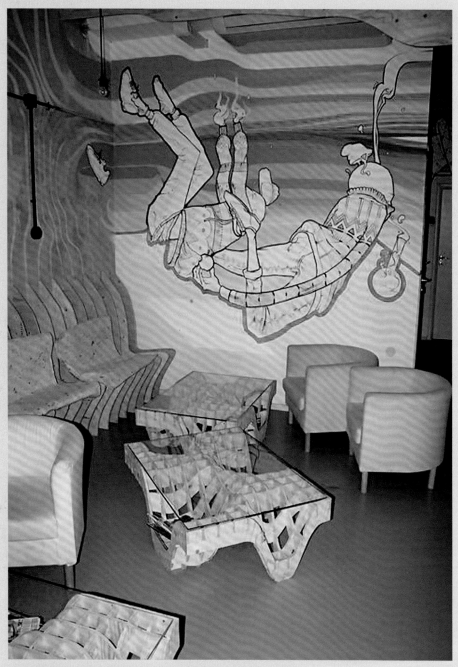

TOP
Ribs arrived on-site in pre-cut sections.

BOTTOM
CNC manufacture ensured perfect interlocking of subsections of the larger ribs.

OPPOSITE TOP LEFT
'Graffiti' murals decorate the new walls to the WCs. Paint continues the lines of the ribs up the existing wall. Plywood ribs become chair structures and CNC test pieces became bases for glass tabletops.

OPPOSITE TOP RIGHT
The bar top transmutes into a table along the wall for standing customers and a seating structure, made more comfortable with loose cushions.

OPPOSITE BOTTOM LEFT
Ribs are cut around existing beams. Centres vary slightly to accommodate local irregularities. Wiring to light fittings and metal fixing angles remain visible.

OPPOSITE BOTTOM RIGHT
CNC manufacture ensures perfect interlocking of subsections.

MYU,
BEIRUT
PAUL KALOUSTIAN

This bar and restaurant is inserted into the shell of an old liquor factory in the heart of Beirut's nightlife district. An existing beam divides the original space into two equal areas but the new proposal introduces two unequal vaults. The larger accommodates the restaurant and the smaller the bar. The long narrow plans ensure that all tables have desirable locations against walls or, in the case of the restaurant, in the substantial central block of banquettes.

The walls of the original space have been left as they were found with rough and decaying plaster. The vaults are constructed of translucent black fabric stretched over a wooden and metal frame. They sit back from the street frontage, to accommodate air conditioning ductwork but, more significantly, to create an entrance area for both sections, which allows the profile of the vaults to be clearly visible and removes the need for their sections to conform to that of the existing entrance arches. The fabric is omitted where the wall between the vaults meets the projecting kitchen block, to allow access between the areas.

The fabric is backlit indirectly by cold cathodes that are directed towards the white painted existing walls, illuminating their textures and imperfections. The light, bounced back onto and through the translucent fabric, may be dimmed for changes in atmosphere.

A 'window' runs the length of both bar and restaurant and this slot is repeated behind the bar where a pre-fabricated steel box, lit from below and supported on the vault ribs, serves as shelving.

RIGHT
A view of the restaurant from the street. Lights are diffused through the translucent vault fabric over the restaurant area and wash the smooth new back wall.

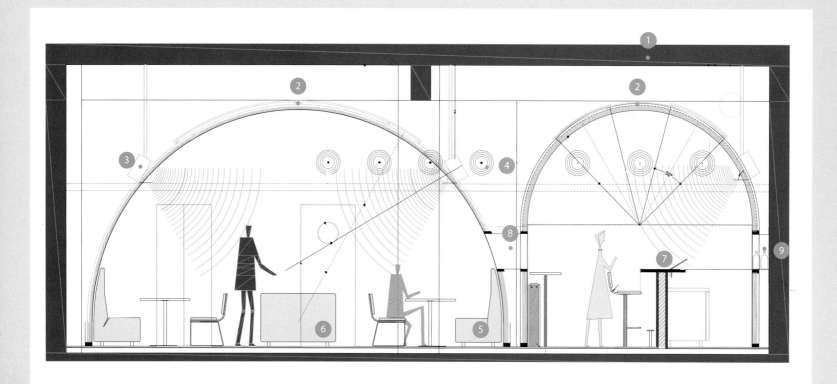

SECTION, SCALE 1:50

OPPOSITE TOP LEFT
Section: restaurant in left vault, bar
in right
1 Existing structure
2 New fabric vault
3 Speakers
4 Air-conditioning duct
5 Wall bench
6 Booth
7 Bar counter
8 'Window' between restaurant and bar
9 Back bar display

OPPOSITE BOTTOM LEFT
The charcoal grey fabric of the new vaults
contrasts with the white painted existing
structure. They are set back from the
existing facade to create an entrance
zone and to accommodate ductwork.

TOP RIGHT
The view from the bar to the restaurant
with an original column to the right.

BOTTOM RIGHT
The slots of the 'window' to the
restaurant and the shelving behind the
counter run the length of the bar. The
imperfections in the original plaster can
be seen through the fabric.

OPPOSITE TOP

The skeleton of the vault during construction. The notch for the cathode lights in the timber frame is visible on the left.

OPPOSITE BOTTOM LEFT

The lights are recessed into the wooden ribs of the vault and reflected off the white painted existing ceiling. Speakers hang on adjustable arms and are visible through the thin fabric.

OPPOSITE BOTTOM RIGHT

Applying the fabric.

RIGHT

Detail section through wooden structure.
1 Threaded steel rods, 10mm (⅜ in)
2 Vertical black-painted steel plate, 4mm (⅛ in)
3 Black-painted steel plate, 4mm (⅛ in)
4 30 x 10mm (1⅛ x ⅜ in) wooden structure painted black

BOTTOM

Detail plan wooden structure
1 Black helioscreen stapled on wooden structure
2 Vertical black-painted steel plate, 4mm (⅛ in)

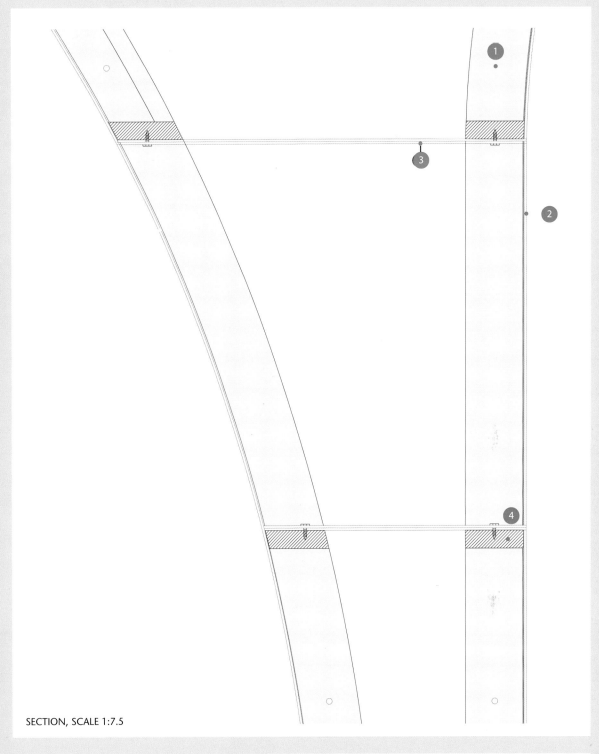

SECTION, SCALE 1:7.5

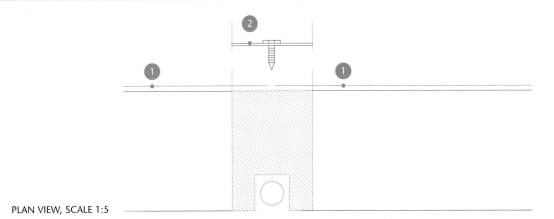

PLAN VIEW, SCALE 1:5

BLUE FROG, MUMBAI
SERIE ARCHITECTS

This 'acoustic lounge', a restaurant, bar and stage is part of a sound recording studio constructed within the shell of a warehouse in a former mill district. The circular booths, which hold from four to ten diners, were constructed on a series of tiers, rising away from the central performance area.

Spaces between the booths are closed to create sloping, backlit surfaces that are the dominant visual element. The designers' intention is that these undulating surfaces should be perceived as a two-dimensional element, with the wall thickness of the booths minimized and the area of the illuminated acrylic resin membranes maximized. To achieve this, they eliminated structural subframing and substituted 19mm (¾ in) blockboard sheets, bent to the radii required for the various sized booths.

Blockboard consists of wooden blocks, or glued strips, to make a single sheet that is faced with plywood. It has significant inherent rigidity and to make the curved sides of the booths one of the plywood veneers was removed and the wooden strips scored to ease bending. When the curved panels were placed in position, the exposed core was re-laminated. The curved form gave extra rigidity to the individual units. The slope, away from the stage, on the upper edges of the booths was cut in situ to ensure a smooth transition between units. The 8mm (⁵⁄₁₆ in) acrylic resin light-diffusing elements were glued to the upper edge and, when lit become the dominant visual element, unifying the space with a single sloping plane.

The acoustic performance of the lounge was a primary consideration. The existing ceiling and perimeter walls are clad in layers of rockwool to absorb low frequency noises and the textured plaster finish on the walls breaks up sound waves.

RIGHT
Sweeping, illuminated bands of colour wrap around the booths. Circles on plan are repeated on the wall surfaces.

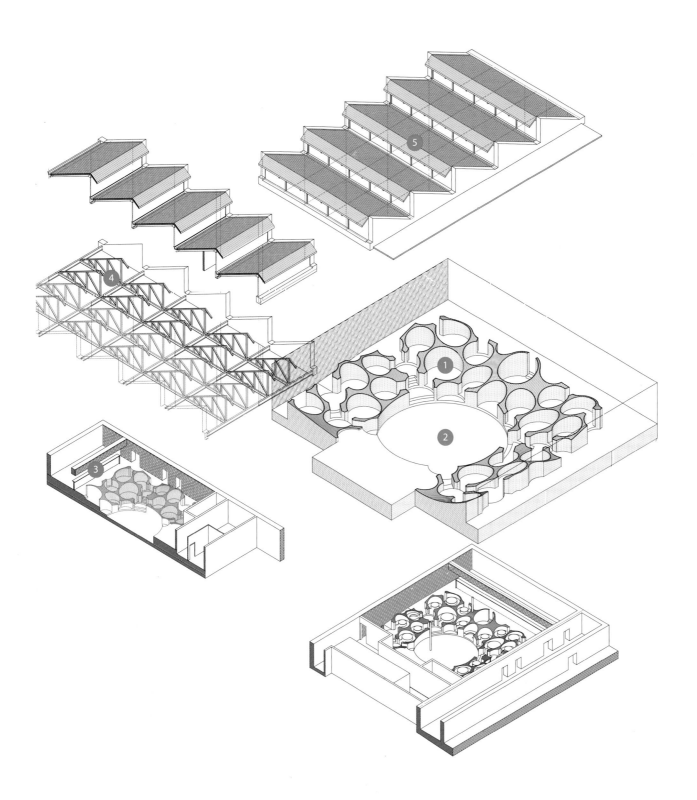

ABOVE
Exploded axonometric
1 Booth seating
2 Stage
3 Private room
4 Existing roof structure
5 Existing rooflights

OPPOSITE TOP LEFT
The circular service grills sit within the grid of surface mouldings on the wall. The segment cut from the tabletop, which eases serving and access, relates visually to the imperfect circles of the ribbons.

OPPOSITE TOP RIGHT
The heavily modelled wall cladding disrupts sound waves.

OPPOSITE BOTTOM
Lights change but the acrylic ribbons remain the dominant element.

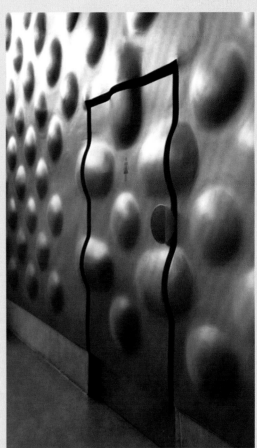

ZEBAR,
SHANGHAI
3GATTI

The ribs that line the walls and ceiling, which define the character of this interior, were conceived and evolved by computer. What the designers describe as an 'amorphous blob', a solid representation of the empty core space was first inserted digitally into the virtual three dimensions of the existing building shell. This 'solid' was then digitally subdivided into slices, which became templates for the ribs.

While CNC computer manufacturing techniques are increasingly used as the most economical and accurate method of cutting large numbers of forms, each with a unique profile, in China labour costs made it more feasible, in this project, to cut the ribs by hand. Additionally, the usual construction technique of prefabricating individual ribs off-site in a specialist workshop before assembly on-site was rejected in favour of a process that allowed precise in-situ shaping of each unique rib. Walls of plasterboard sheets on timber subframing were sequentially built to fill the entire cross section of the existing space and the profile of the void, unique to the location of each, was projected on to it. The redundant area of plasterboard, defined by the projection, was then cut out by hand. The remaining area of wall became the rib. The designers were surprised by the speed with which this ad hoc procedure was carried out and very satisfied with the quality of finish on the completed ribs.

Each 100mm (4 in) wide rib was finished with a white epoxy coating, as is the line that connects the points where each rib meets the concrete floor, to create the illusion of a continuous element running around all horizontal and vertical planes. The dark areas of floor are black stained concrete inset with small black stones. The organic form of the bar counter is finished with the same black render on an expanded metal lath, supported on a metal sub-frame.

RIGHT
The VIP area looking towards the stage.
A rib supports spotlights.

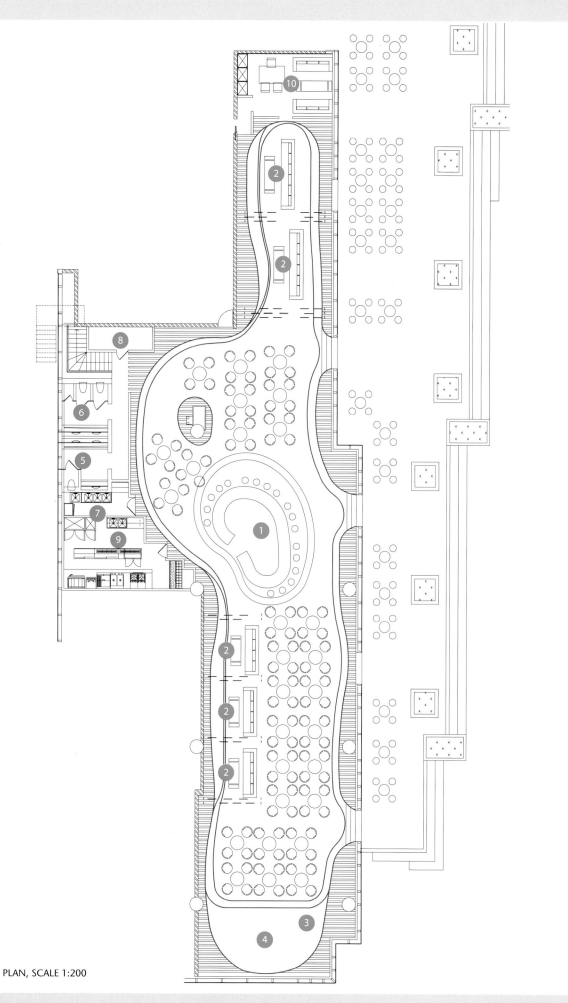

LEFT
1 Bar
2 VIP room
3 DJ
4 Stage
5 Male WCs
6 Female WCs
7 Dressing room
8 Machine room
9 Kitchen
10 Office

OPPOSITE TOP RIGHT
Ribs adapt to support seating in the bar area and appear to wrap continuously around all surfaces. Light sources of varying intensities, concealed between them, punctuate the length of the room.

OPPOSITE MIDDLE LEFT
Digitally defined ribs filled the spaces between the new internal volume and the existing shell.

OPPOSITE BOTTOM LEFT
The profile of each rib was projected on to a plasterboard wall that filled the whole cross section of the room and the redundant middle section was cut out in-situ.

OPPOSITE BOTTOM RIGHT
Skilled labour ensured a high quality of finish for complex elements constructed entirely on-site.

PLAN, SCALE 1:200

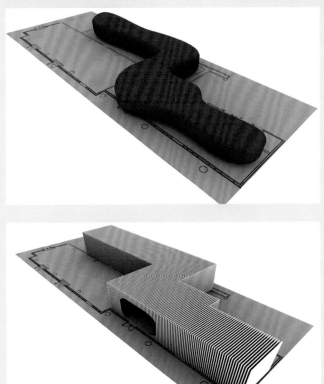

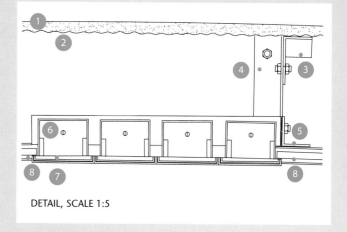

DETAIL, SCALE 1:5

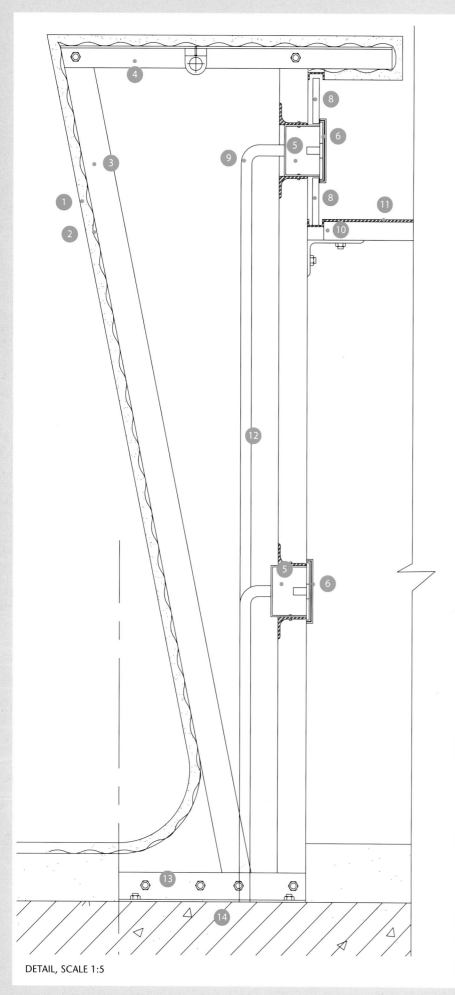

DETAIL, SCALE 1:5

LEFT & TOP
Bar front, plan and section
1 Sand and cement render
2 Expanded metal lath
3 Vertical steel framing
4 Horizontal steel framing
5 Steel support bracket
6 Socket box
7 Socket box cover
8 9mm (⅜ in) acrylic sheet
9 40 x 25mm (1½ x 1 in) steel angle support
10 Steel angle support
11 Brushed stainless steel worktop on 3mm plywood
12 Electrical conduit
13 Steel framing bolted to floor
14 Concrete subfloor

TOP
The bar was also constructed in-situ.

BOTTOM
The roughly textured bar front shares the organic lines of the smooth white ribs.

FACTORY 251,
MANCHESTER
BEN KELLY DESIGN

One of the most influential interiors of the early 1980s was The Hacienda nightclub in Manchester, created by Ben Kelly Design for an anarchic consortium made up of the owners of Factory Records and a few of their recording artists. It became the prototype for those clubs catering for congregations of dance-music fans and a cultural phenomenon, albeit at the cost of sound business practice. Its mythic reputation ensured protests when it was demolished and replaced by an apartment block but its legend survived and when the client for this project, who had been a Hacienda enthusiast, acquired the nearby building that had housed the headquarters of the now defunct Factory Records he asked BKD to design a new bar/club over its three floors.

While the new building broadly shared the industrial aesthetic of the original club, its spaces were more modestly proportioned and lacked significant existing elements. Had they wished to do so, BKD could not have replicated the original but they were more enthusiastic about the opportunity to make variations on some of its most characteristic elements.

Existing windows on each level are bricked up and plastered. Lighting is provided by what the designers refer to as a 'raft' of ceiling-mounted cold cathode neon tubes and the intensely backlit panels of the bar fronts that form the dominant and identifying element on each floor. Patterns created for the bar front panels are reminiscent of devices used in the original club and in Factory Records memorabilia. Assembly involves comprehensible techniques typical of basic industrial construction.

The reworking of Hacienda detailing is typified by the short lengths of neon – mounted on the existing column in the centre of the ground-level dance floor and protected by clear toughened glass – that refer to the diagonal stripes, themselves inspired by graphic industrial warning devices that alerted dancers to, and adorned, existing columns in the Hacienda.

RIGHT
Ground floor: The diagonal motifs of the original club are reinterpreted in the diagonal fluorescent tubes set behind the painted metal mesh of the bar front and the glass panels fixed to the existing column. The glazed tiles of the DJ box on the left sit comfortably in the surviving industrial aesthetic.

OPPOSITE TOP LEFT

The original Hacienda nightclub (by day) with its trademark stripes and colours.

OPPOSITE TOP RIGHT

Protective glass panels are bolted to the existing steel columns, with spacers to accommodate the fluorescent tube diagonals.

OPPOSITE BOTTOM

First floor: The laminated yellow and white diagonal stripes of the bar front are lit from beneath the counter top by short, intense 'Stick-Lites'. Ventilation equipment and radiators are exposed. OSB panels cover the windows.

TOP RIGHT

1 Entrance
2 Reception
3 Dance floor
4 Existing column
5 Bar
6 DJ
7 Sound box
8 Stage
9 Stair to upper floors and fire escape
10 Fire escape to exterior

MIDDLE RIGHT

1 Access and fire escape stair
2 Dance floor
3 Bar
4 DJ
5 Sunken seating
6 Void over reception
7 Void over entrance
8 Fire escape
9 WCs

BOTTOM RIGHT

1 Dance floor
2 Bar
3 DJ
4 Escape and access
5 Plant
6 Void over first floor
7 Void over entrance

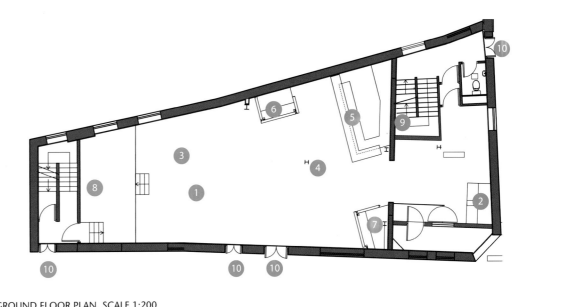

GROUND FLOOR PLAN, SCALE 1:200

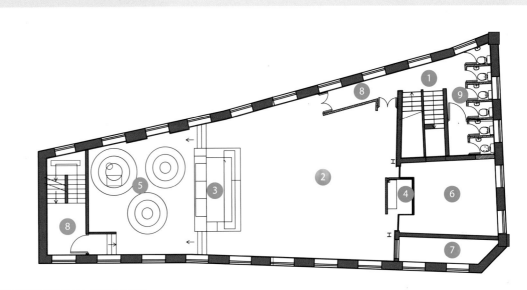

FIRST FLOOR PLAN, SCALE 1:200

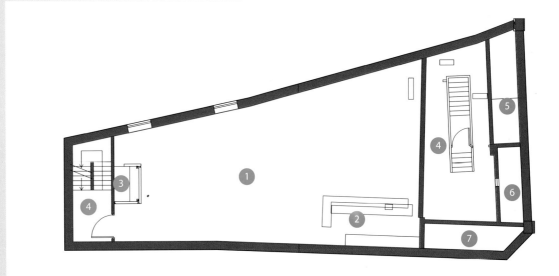

SECOND FLOOR PLAN, SCALE 1:200

TOP

Top floor: The blue of the backlit plywood panels that clad the bar front is repeated throughout the level. The red wall behind the DJ box relates to the lower floors.

BOTTOM

The apertures in the unpainted plywood panel are inspired by the record sleeve that Kelly designed in collaboration with legendary graphic designer Peter Saville.

OPPOSITE

A standard assembly for the bar counter allows front panels to be located in front (on the bottom level) to hide the steel angle structure and behind (on the upper floors) to respond to the industrial aesthetic.

1 Flat mild steel strap, to support bar, top welded to main 75 x 50 x 6mm (3 x 2 x ¼ in) mild steel angle upright

2 6mm (¼ in) fabricated bracket bolted to upright and fixed back to bar carcass for stability

3 75 x 50 x 6mm (3 x 2 x ¼ in) angle bolted to main upright, with 6mm stainless steel spacers, to support fascia panel

4 75 x 50 x 6mm (3 x 2 x ¼ in) angle foot rail bolted to floor bracket

5 6mm mild steel fabricated bracket bolted to existing floor and main upright

6 Bar carcass

7 Fascia panel

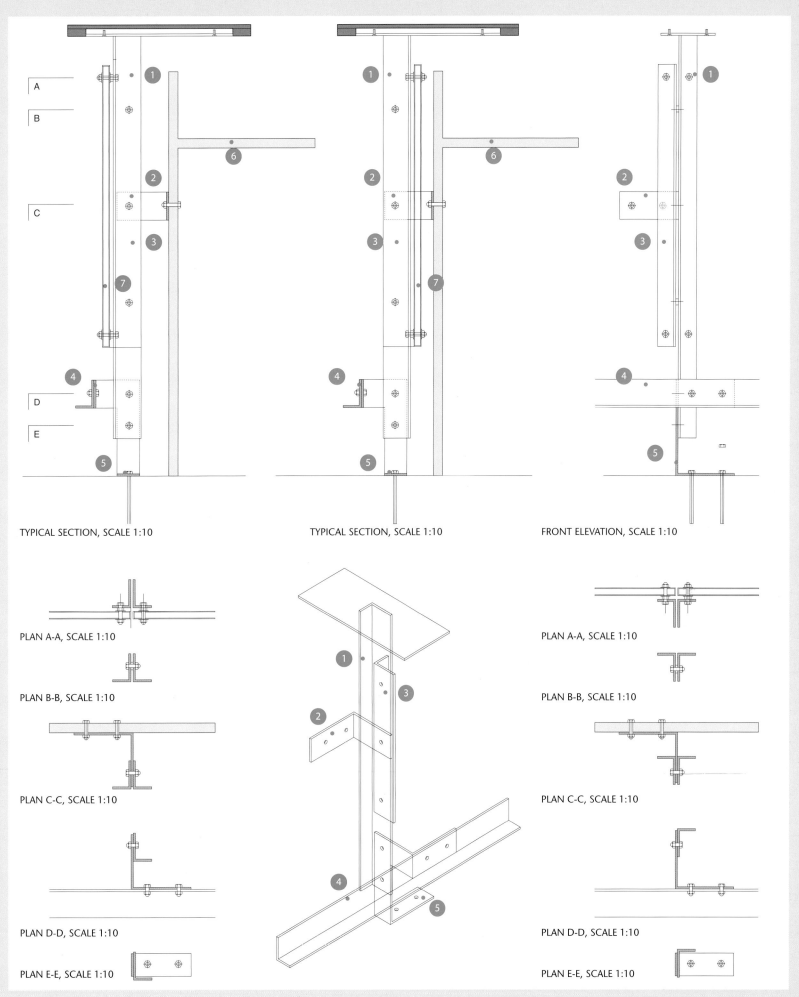

TYPICAL SECTION, SCALE 1:10

TYPICAL SECTION, SCALE 1:10

FRONT ELEVATION, SCALE 1:10

A

B

C

D

E

PLAN A-A, SCALE 1:10

PLAN B-B, SCALE 1:10

PLAN C-C, SCALE 1:10

PLAN D-D, SCALE 1:10

PLAN E-E, SCALE 1:10

PLAN A-A, SCALE 1:10

PLAN B-B, SCALE 1:10

PLAN C-C, SCALE 1:10

PLAN D-D, SCALE 1:10

PLAN E-E, SCALE 1:10

DESIGN BAR 2010, STOCKHOLM
JONAS WAGELL

The empty shells of major exhibition spaces tend to be conceived as neutral backdrops for the diversity of temporary installations that are concerned with maximizing their individual impact. The shared hospitality areas, provided by the exhibition organizers have a captive audience but, although relieved of direct competition with commercial rivals, they are required to give the event its own identity, to establish and sustain it as a worthwhile investment for exhibitors.

This bar was designed for the five days of the 2010 Stockholm Furniture Fair and owes more to the principles and techniques of stage and graphic design than those used for more permanent constructions. There were two areas, a public place serving food and drink, packed with tables, chairs and small-scale exhibits, and another more private space, designated as a VIP lounge and reserved for business meetings. The two areas shared the theme of Forest and Industry, acknowledging two essential cornerstones of Swedish furniture manufacture.

Their shared perimeter was defined by a floor-to-ceiling curtain against which two-dimensional shapes cut from MDF, symbolizing mountains and factories, were set at floor level. These were layered on plan to increase the perceived depth of the 'landscape' and to conceal between them low-level light sources that washed their surfaces. Where connected to those in front of and behind them they became a deeper, composite and more stable structure. Cut-outs suspended from the underside of the roof and augmented with white and grey balloons suggested clouds. A change of colour transformed 'clouds' into the 'bushes' that, with 'tree trunks' laden with balloon 'fruit', subdivided the floor area. Suspended green plastic horticultural netting hung from the ceiling provided additional subdivision. Both bar and VIP lounge were carpeted. Furniture and fittings were selected from the ranges produced by Swedish manufacturers.

TOP
The quieter VIP lounge refers to forests and mountains. The carpet pattern and 'trees' define areas for conversation.

BOTTOM
New Swedish products fulfil practical functions.

OPPOSITE TOP
In the cafe two-dimensional shapes and balloons suggest mountains, factories, clouds and trees and obscure typical trade-show clutter.

OPPOSITE BOTTOM LEFT
1 VIP area
2 Public area
3 Bar servery
4 Two-dimensional MDF backdrops and divisions
5 Floor pattern
6 Suspended balloon 'clouds'

OPPOSITE BOTTOM RIGHT
Visible panel joints and fixings are accepted. Triangular braces support the tree forms and additional layers at floor level give them breadth and weight for greater stability.

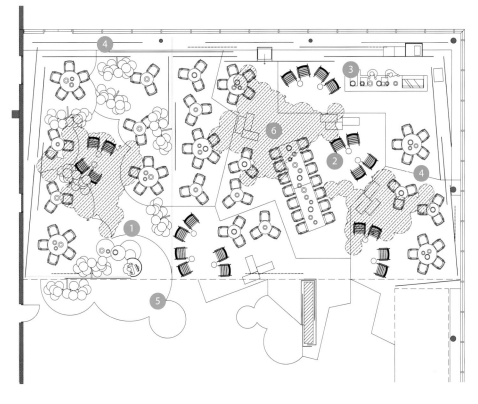

PLAN, SCALE 1:400

DESIGN BAR 2011, STOCKHOLM
KATRIN GREILING

In the Design Bar of 2010 (see page 78), the elements that defined the bar obscured, as far as was feasible, evidence of the existing fabric of the exhibition hall. For the same exhibition in the same context a year later, the existing elements were allowed a much greater presence. Small-scale, brightly coloured additions and the ostensibly ad hoc techniques used in their production were deployed against the greys of the engineered and machine-made structure that contained them. The territory of the bar was defined by an existing area of wooden floor and translucent plastic sheets, suspended from the roof structure, that acted as walls and intermediaries between the inflated scale of the original shell and the furniture pieces that defined the bar's temporary character and function.

Small round tables provided places for groups and perhaps more private conversations. Long tables with benches, located beneath hanging 'roof'/lighting structures, accommodated individuals and encouraged informal interaction. Wooden loungers with suspended cardboard hoods provided retreats and resting places. Long cushions, lashed together with ropes, represented the most extreme reductive detailing.

The 'roof'/lighting structures over tables and the hoods over loungers were assembled from cardboard sheets, fixed over rudimentary timber dowel structures and suspended on thin wires from the roof structure high above. The simplicity and clarity of construction sat comfortably with the light touch that characterized all other new elements. The lounger hoods perhaps represent the most elegant example of the approach since the single supporting rod that passes through the top of each allows them to find a consistent hanging angle that is determined by their shared centre of gravity.

The plywood sheets used in the construction of the 'hut' that contained the kitchen and food servery is tonally close to that of the existing wooden floor. The base structure for the 'Pineapple' bar and the hood over it were truncated cones of flexible plywood, drilled to receive projecting 200mm (8 in) long wooden battens with rounded ends over which yellow stretch fabric was drawn and stapled in position. A section of the front was omitted for access and a corresponding length of the varnished plywood counter-top lifted for access.

RIGHT

An existing wooden floor and suspended translucent plastic sheets establish the area of the bar. The servery 'hut' and yellow bar provide its focus and the furniture pieces provide for different degrees of social interaction.

TOP LEFT
Colourful and clearly ephemeral elements counterpoint existing elements. The yellow stretch fabric of the bar is shaped by dowels that project from the upper and lower truncated conical core structures.

TOP RIGHT
To make the lighting 'roofs' wooden dowels are slid through holes in the cardboard sheet and held in position by secondary dowels inserted at the appropriate angle. The overtly casual method accepts and excuses the slight and inevitable sagging.

BOTTOM LEFT
A continuous wire allows the hoods to find a common hanging angle, determined by their centre of gravity.

TOP
The plywood cladding of the food 'hut' is tonally close to the wooden floor. White adhesive lettering provides information.

RIGHT
Translucent plastic sheets, hung from the roof, mark the perimeter, filter views and diffuse light.

LA CANTINE DE LA MÉNAGERIE DE VERRE, PARIS
MATALI CRASSET

The 'Glass Menagerie' is an established multi-disciplinary space in Paris described as 'a research laboratory' dedicated to contemporary dance. In this redesign of its reception space, which doubles as a cafe and occasional performance area, the impact of new elements on the existing building was kept to a minimum and the efficient use of materials maximized.

The solution reinterprets the familiar precedent of the trestle to support both chairs and tables so that these, when disassembled, may be stored in a purpose-built corner structure. All new elements, with the exception of the blue pouffes, are cut from 25mm (1 in) birch-veneered plywood sheets and connected with interlocking slotted joints. When loaded, the angle of the trestle legs is determined by the canvas strip that connects them at base level.

The tabletops are assembled from the remnants left after the trestle cutting process. The rounded corners that are a consequence of thickening and strengthening the corners of the comparatively thin trestle frames give a distinctive edge to the tops and define individual space allocation on shared tables. Tops sit comparatively low to the floor, to encourage informality and conviviality.

The chair seats and backrests are produced as a composite unit made up of three pieces of plywood, the curved intermediate piece being the only element in the whole family of components not cut from a flat sheet. Slotted ribs beneath the seat act as housings for corresponding slots in the trestles.

The pouffes consist of a fabric cover over a dense foam block. Velcro strips provide connections between base and back. Handle loops encourage users to move them. Other off-cuts from trestle production sit on top of them and serve as tabletops. Projecting lugs provide handles.

TOP
Individual components of tables and chairs are clearly visible. Off-cuts from trestle production become serrated-edged tabletops.

BOTTOM
Fabric-covered foam-cored pouffes may be repositioned for different activities. Off-cuts from trestle production convert them from seats to tabletops.

ABOVE
The cafe area is defined by walls, columns and servery. The plywood storage unit wraps around an existing column.

RIGHT
Demounted elements of tables and chairs are stacked on the storage unit. Slots in the seat rib will fix the angle for trestle legs.

KADE, AMERSFOORT
STUDIO MAKKINK & BEY

KAdE is not a conventional museum with a permanent collection but a flexible space for temporary exhibitions. The designers were asked to provide an interior that could be transformed quickly and easily to deal with changing content. They responded by producing a series of multi-functional furniture pieces that could be moved and used throughout the building and which could adapt to users' needs and preferences. Their pieces acknowledge the design principles of Gerrit Rietveld who was responsible for the earlier De Zonnehof exhibition space, which KAdE replaces.

It is the furniture pieces that bring character to the existing interior spaces, whose blandness is accepted and exploited as an effective foil for the complex furniture that has been generated by detailed consideration of function.

The cafe is multi-purpose, used for eating, drinking, reading or working. The single-sided servery is hard against the wall so that its activities are integrated in and wholly visible from the sitting area, which is shared by visitors and staff who may choose to sit, individually or communally, at a long table that echoes the materials and construction techniques of the reception desk or at the smaller tables on the terrace. Or they may choose individual chairs, each with an integral horizontal work surface.

There are two chair types. The KAde model, in which swivelling Eames plastic seats are mounted on a wooden base, offers options. Groups may turn to create a shared space. Individuals may turn away to find privacy. While the simple, clearly articulated, forms of the KAdE base reflects the spirit of Rietveld's construction it is the Amersfoort chair that utilizes variations on the butt joints that characterized his 'Red Blue' chair although generous upholstery is substituted for its unpadded plywood planes.

ABOVE
The single-sided servery is built against the wall. The frame of the black-upholstered Amersfoort chair uses the butt jointing technique of Rietveld's Red Blue chair.

RIGHT
Eames plastic seat units swivel on top of wooden bases that reflect Rietveld's direct construction principles. Wooden horizontal surfaces, supported off the base on brackets, act as armrests and tables.

ABOVE LEFT
Rietveld/Eames hybrid chairs share the area with the long communal table. Movable display cases bring exhibition material into the space.

ABOVE RIGHT
The mechanics of the servery are exposed to the room to encourage informal integration between staff and visitors.

BELOW
1 Cafe
2 Kitchen preparation and servery
3 Wooden communal table
4 KAdE chair
5 Amersfoort chair
6 Display cabinets
7 Carpet-tile squares
8 Storage/temporary partition
9 Movable storage wall
10 Lockable storage wall
11 Work table
12 Chair/sofa
13 Storage

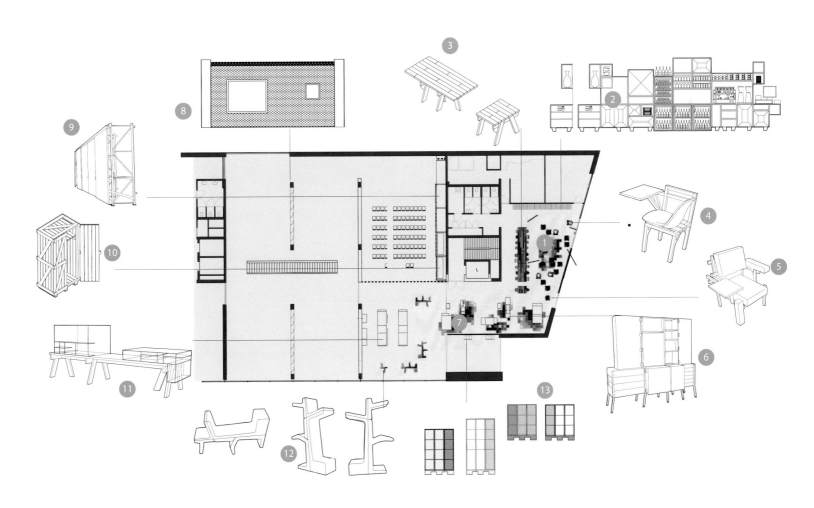

DIE KUNSTBAR, COLOGNE
SAQ

The site of this temporary bar is close to Cologne cathedral and the genesis of the project is very particular to its physical and cultural context, but the creative approach that shaped it is relevant to any interior that relies on the installation of evocative and provocative elements rather than complex construction to establish its identity. Elements are designed to prompt customers', perhaps subliminal, response to an implied narrative, the precise details of which are not necessarily shared by any who experience it.

The project engages users' imaginations with familiar materials and comprehensible making techniques but the bedrock of its success is the logical way it occupies its space. One long wall of the main bar area, and a section of the roof abutting it, is wholly glazed but the focus of the interior is a multiple-video installation on the opposite wall, which suggests that the divine, all-seeing eye has been replaced by a digital one. While the placement of screens is deliberate the distribution of power cables is expedient and the edge of the black painted wall area, left ragged by the roller strokes, confirms that, in this case, spontaneous communication is more important than overwrought perfection. The broken edge also helps integrate the black and white wall masses and suggests the visual texture of a moulded picture frame.

The bar counter, which is situated in a secondary windowless space, is assembled with the rough wood and simple fabricating techniques more normally used to make crates for the transportation of artwork. The same principles are used for the side tables, topped with glass, and the benches, topped with foam and skins, that fill the perimeter zone, which is defined by the roof glazing. The pastel upholstery of the conventional chairs is complemented by the colours of the skins, attached by buttons, that are draped over them.

TOP
Coloured light tints and binds new and existing surfaces. The slash of white light on the floor and beyond balances the fragments on the screens.

MIDDLE
The glass-topped bar counter uses crate construction techniques. Coloured lights upgrade the air-conditioning ducts.

BOTTOM
Simple materials and fabrication make a friendly object.

TOP
The layout of new elements follows the curve of the existing plan. The layout of chairs makes it clear that contemplation is more important than conversation.

RIGHT
The expedient distribution of power cables, the ragged edged paintwork and the skins casually draped over conventional chairs establish an aesthetic at odds with the existing shell.

MS CAFÉ,
LODZ
WUNDERTEAM

The Lodz museum of art houses exhibits from the nineteenth and twentieth centuries in what was a nineteenth century residential building. The designers were asked to improve public awareness of the museum and to provide a cafe and bookshop that would act as a social space. They signalled the existence of something different behind the traditional street facade by glazing both ends of the original entrance corridor. The cafe and bookshop are located to the left of the entrance and the galleries and a new information desk and ticket kiosk to the right.

The raw finishes and clearly legible construction techniques of the new internal elements contrast with the delicate and colourful detailing of the original building. Their forms refer to the museum's functions. The faceted cladding panels of plywood, on an OSB carcass, and backlit white acrylic, on a plywood base, conceal the ergonomic priority of the working bar and suggest a fragment of monumental sculpture. The triangular geometry of both the plywood and acrylic panels is echoed in the Grcic bar stools and the suspended gantry, which also has a visual affinity with the structure of the glazed box of the bookshop.

The soft, thick upholstery of the bar seating is supported on layered plywood backs and bases that are intended to suggest the crates used in the transportation of works of art. Rough materials, crude construction and wheels signal that they have no pretensions to become permanent elements in competition with the original splendours of the building.

The seating cubes, also raised on wheels, are positioned with no apparent regard for the existing windows, also setting them distinctly apart from the original architecture. The thin, bright yellow and red folded metal tables that bisect them contrast not only with the original architecture but the raw plywood and soft seating.

RIGHT
A view from within a plywood booth in the first bar area towards the entrance and bookshop. The reddish plywood of the booths and bar finds some tonal common ground with the moulded ceiling but the construction of the booths belongs to a wholly different detailing language. A vertical metal sheet supports the midpoint of the yellow and red metal tables.

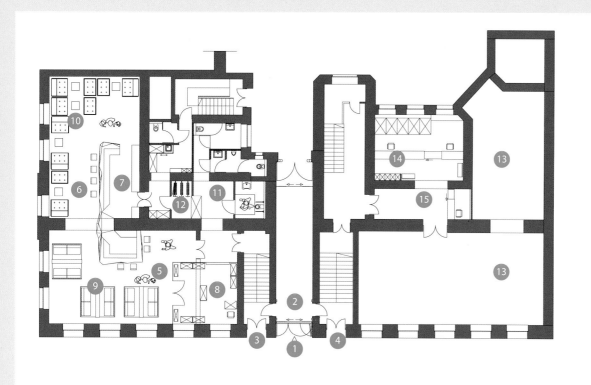

PLAN, SCALE 1:200

LEFT
Plan
1 Existing archway
2 New main entrance
3 New secondary entrance to bars
and bookshop
4 New secondary entrance to exhibition
spaces
5 Cafe 1
6 Cafe 2
7 Bar counter
8 Bookshop
9 Seating cubes
10 Upholstery/plywood seats
11 WCs
12 Cloakroom
13 Exhibition rooms
14 Lobby
15 Cloakroom

BOTTOM
In the second bar area the space is less
crowded in response to lighter ceiling
mouldings. The clear expression of
detailing in the new sofas and benches
sets it apart from both the original
moulded surfaces and the smooth
factory finishes of the new proprietary
elements, the light fittings, bar gantry
and ventilation duct, which are equally
distinct from the original architecture.

TOP
Front elevation of bar counter.

MIDDLE
End elevations of bar counter.

BOTTOM
The geometry and colour of the bar stools relate easily to the triangular facets and the backlit acrylic panels. The shadow of the plywood framing behind the acrylic is visible. The location of the wheeled booths does not relate to the existing windows. Stencilled lettering mimics that on transportation crates.

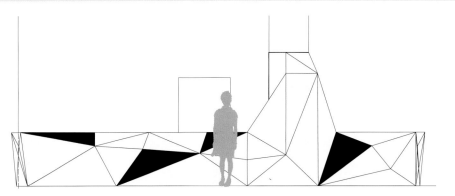

FRONT ELEVATION, SCALE 1:75

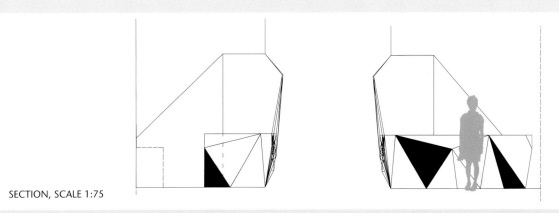

SECTION, SCALE 1:75

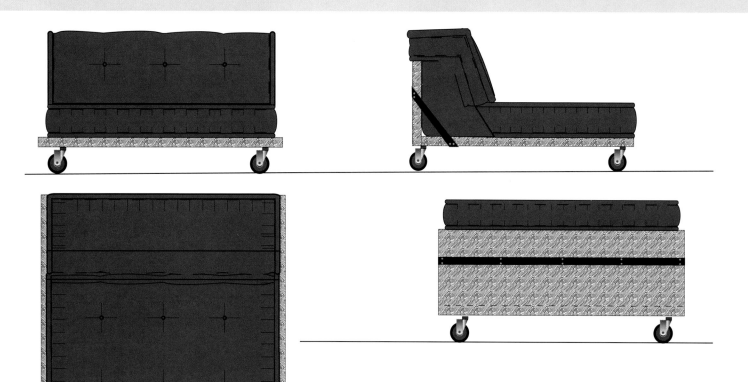

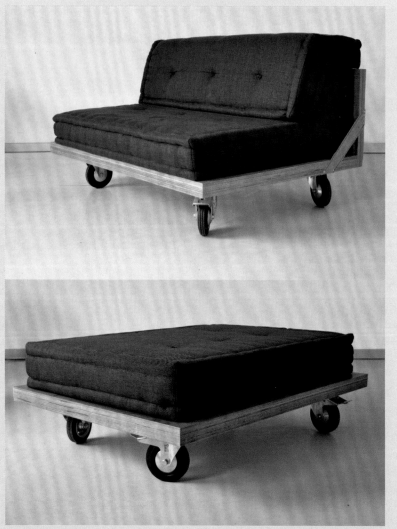

TOP
Plan and elevations of Cafe 2 seating

LEFT
The simple construction of both seating types is exposed and wholly comprehensible. The angled strip stiffens the corner.

OPPOSITE TOP LEFT
Section through seating cube: cafe 2
1 Plywood sheet
2 Upholstered seat
3 Bent sheet steel table: ends and top
4 Bent sheet steel central support
5 Casters

OPPOSITE TOP RIGHT
In the cloakroom the red element slides under the counter to allow access for attendants. Garments are stored behind glass doors.

OPPOSITE MIDDLE LEFT
Base fixing for sheet metal table
1 Vertical end section
2 Continuous steel angle screwed to plywood base
3 Steel clamping piece bolted to angle
4 Plywood base

OPPOSITE MIDDLE RIGHT
Cross section through table
1 Table top
2 Central support: radiused top and bottom to increase rigidity
3 Plate bolted to angle
4 Screws to fix angle

OPPOSITE BOTTOM
Elevation of sheet metal table
1 Continuous metal ends and top
2 Corner radiused to increase rigidity
3 Steel central support
4 See detail above

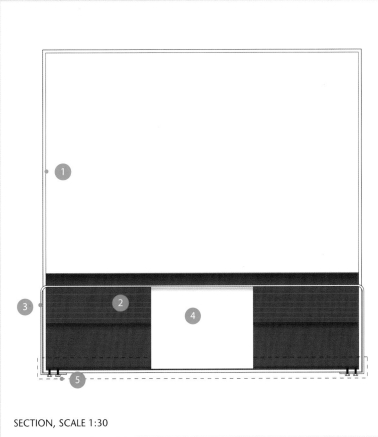

SECTION, SCALE 1:30

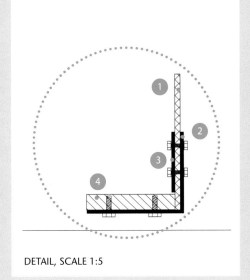

DETAIL, SCALE 1:5

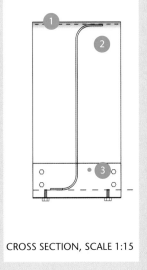

CROSS SECTION, SCALE 1:15

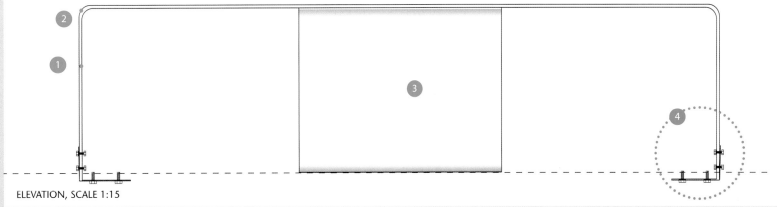

ELEVATION, SCALE 1:15

PLUK, HAARLEM
TJEP

Health food cafes are predisposed to look dull, perhaps to confirm their commitment to their customers' well-being rather than their self-gratification. Pluk owners and designers were agreed that the interior must suggest the possibility of self-indulgence, prompted by their philosophy that 99 percent of healthy eating leaves room for 1 percent 'unhealthy junk'.

The Pluk interior does conform to health food cafes' tendency to fetishize ingredients and uses the colour palette suggested by fruits and vegetables deemed beneficial but exploits them with a wit and panache that suggests a menu offering something more than a means to self-denial. The acrylic counter front and bulkhead above it are the defining elements. Deep, frameless containers for ingredients are organized into three colour groups, reddish pink, rich dark green and pale yellow ochre. The transparent panels are tinted in sympathy with the produce they contain. The fruits and vegetables on display are artificial to avoid the need for regular replacement, which is difficult because different varieties wilt at different rates and leave the composition of the cafe's primary visual element to chance.

Computer-generated images of ingredients decorate the wall behind the bench seat, which is colour matched to the pinkish red of the counter front. The recognizable originals are extruded upwards so that the least tempting adopt the melting consistency characteristic of more hedonistic foods. Broccoli appears to have an affinity with the melting chocolate next to it. The distorted and distended red chillies that decorate the bottom of the stairs, also varnished pink and which lead to the lavatories, confirm a more stimulating set of ingredients than is found in the conventional health food menu.

TOP
The tinted acrylic counter front and bulkhead reservoirs contain colour graded artificial fruits and vegetables. The dominant colour is the pinkish red, found also in the bench seat and the chillies that point to the stairs.

MIDDLE
The ingredients behind the tinted acrylic appear to float on their own juices.

BOTTOM
Plan
1 Entrance
2 Produce display containers

3 Wall display
4 High table
5 Tables
6 Bench seating
7 Preparation area
8 Servery counters
9 Fresh produce storage
10 Stairs to WCs
11 Storage

OPPOSITE
Images of ingredients sit slightly proud of the wall behind the bench seating. The image of chocolate, representing the 'permissible 1 percent' indulgence, is smaller than those of healthier foods.

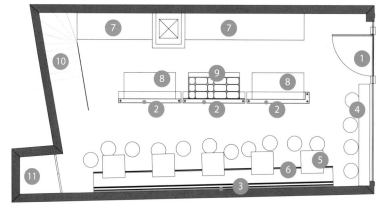

PLAN, SCALE 1:100

POLKA GELATO, LONDON
VONSUNG

This little cafe in the centre of London was created to launch a chain that will specialize in luxurious, exotically flavoured, handmade ice creams, good coffee and tea. The designers were also involved in the development and design of the visual identity, signage and website. In plotting the brand strategy the clichés of ice cream parlour design, bright colours and laminate surfaces, were quickly rejected. It was decided that the sharp colours of the different ice cream flavours would provide the only bright colours and act as the focus of the interior, engaging customers as they crossed the threshold, and that all other components should conform to a complementary monochromatic palette. Responsibility for the total branding allowed the designers to ensure that graphic devices on tubs and beakers provided harmonious small-scale visual details.

The wall finish, a lime/cement render, was cast in-situ using plywood shuttering panels and, while some areas where the surface was not perfect after the removal of the shuttering were repaired by hand, the rough texture and tonal variations suggests something of the consistency of traditional, handmade ice cream. The implication that the concrete render is a solid wall, rather than a finish applied to existing brick, is underpinned by the circular, regularly spaced white plastic inserts that represent the holes left when the bolts, which hold the shuttering in position, are removed and have some affinity with the round white paper tubs and cups. The polished concrete floor and the smooth painted plaster ceiling provide tonally compatible practical finishes. The lighting, concealed in a recess where the ceiling meets the back wall, boosts the colours of the ice cream in the serving counter.

Furniture is black or white and exclusively circular, like the graphic patterns on the logo-ed tubs and cups that, with the ice cream colours, enliven the tiny black tabletops. The large black upholstered seating unit forms a central hub and can accommodate tightly packed customers without obliging them to confront each other. The angle of the white plastic stools suggests the shape and slump of ice cream extruded by a hand squeezed scoop.

TOP
The glass menu board sets a simple font and graphic symbols against the rough textured wall behind.

BOTTOM
Rough wall texture suggests that of hand made ice cream and the worn walls of an ancient workplace in which artisans might follow traditional recipes The white plastic wall inserts relate to the tubs' graphic decoration.

TOP LEFT
Black and white furniture translates the graphic identity into three dimensions.

TOP RIGHT
The colours of the ice creams, the illuminated counter and the concealed perimeter lighting on the back wall are the focus of the room.

BOTTOM
1 Entrance
2 Counter
3 Shelf
4 Cash register
5 Coffee machine
6 Menu board
7 Stools and tables
8 Upholstered seat
9 WC
10 Washroom
11 Stair to basement

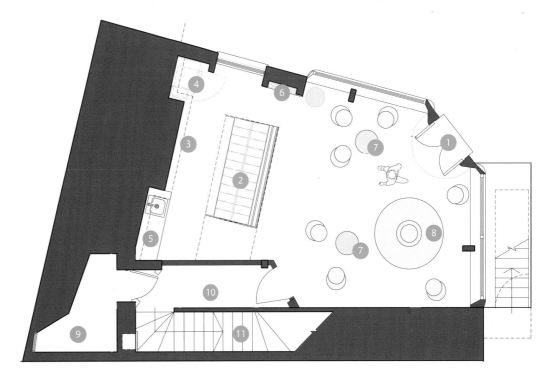

GROUND FLOOR PLAN, SCALE 1:100

RECESS,
NEW YORK
SCALAR ARCHITECTURE

Recess sells frozen yogurt during summer days and coffee in winter and at night. The designers set out to create an interior that could operate successfully for both markets and were particularly keen to avoid the bright, white and glossy finishes and fittings that have emerged as the generic solution to frozen yogurt bars. The interior is characterized by inclined planes and the designers signalled this to the street by substituting new, angled window frames for the existing vertical units. Internal walls slope at angles that are prompted by ergonomic and anthropometric considerations. They offer inclined back supports for wall benches and sloping planes against which standing customers may lean while their tubs and cups are supported on short cantilevered trays.

The inclined planes sit proud of the existing walls and columns and the gaps between them conceal light sources that wash the walls above them. Sheet materials used as a floor finish are cut to eliminate their rectangularity and the angled junctions emphasize their individuality and suggest an undulating surface. The solid end supports of the table, which dominates the centre of the room, lean at a rakish angle. The serving counter is broken into four sections, which meet at angles on plan and are vertically and horizontally unaligned so that they read as a collection of similar but independent volumes.

The visual complexity of the room is enhanced by the strong, irregular pattern of Plyboo, a renewable laminate composite made from fast-growing bamboo, which is used for flooring, furniture and wall cladding, to a height of approximately 2m (6 ½ ft). Above this, walls and ceiling are clad in a brown recycled polymer fabric that is tonally close to the darker areas in the Plyboo. It is also used for the screens that diffuse natural and artificial light and make angled junctions between windows and ceiling. The centre section of the ceiling is raised and contains lengths of irregularly twisted and folded recycled stainless steel sheet, which form troughs to conceal the LED light sources that wash the ceiling. The colour of light may be varied to suit time of day, the season of the year and the music played.

TOP
The faceted awnings and angled windows and door handles are modest preludes to the extravagances of the interior.

BOTTOM
The sloping and fragmented planes of the central table and the counter are reflected and further abstracted in the twisted and folded steel lighting troughs hung in the ceiling recess.

TOP

1 Entrance
2 Leaning walls
3 High-backed wall bench
4 Table
5 Low-backed window bench
6 Counter
7 Preparation
8 WC

MIDDLE

Section AA

1 Folded metal ceiling fins
2 Window bench
3 Counter units
4 Staff access
5 Wall bench

BOTTOM

Section BB

1 Folded metal ceiling fins
2 Leaning wall
3 Table
4 Counter
5 Preparation

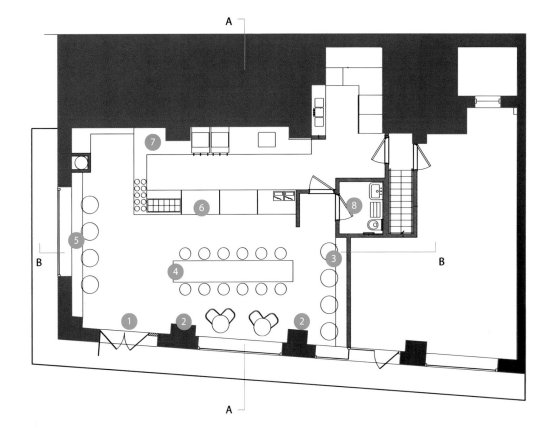

PLAN, SCALE 1:100

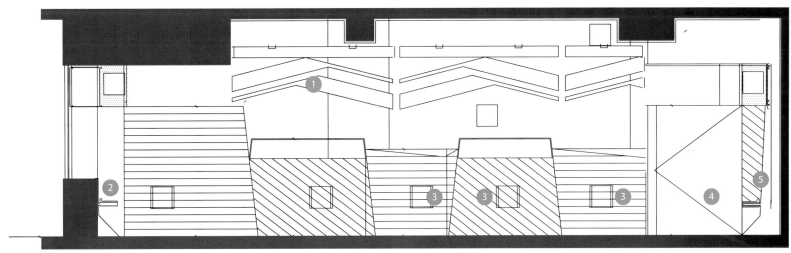

SECTION A-A, SCALE 1:50

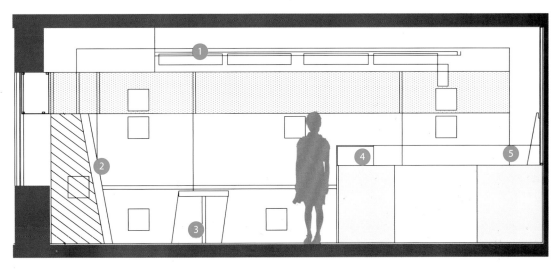

SECTION B-B, SCALE 1:50

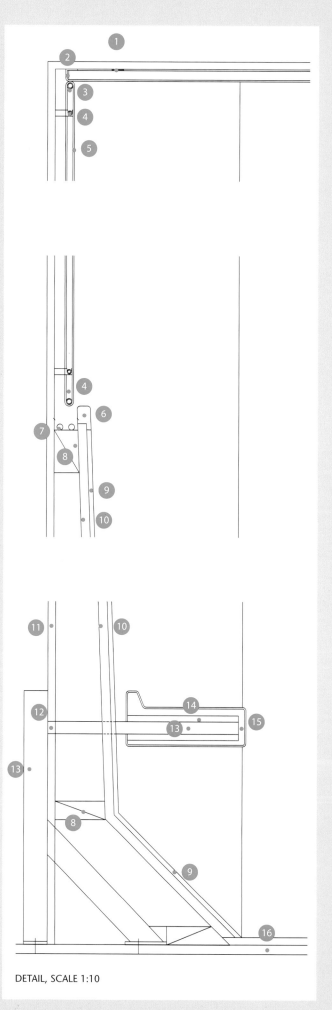

DETAIL, SCALE 1:10

OPPOSITE LEFT

Sloping Plyboo sheets make a backrest for the cantilevered bench. Recycled polymer fabric covers the upper wall, the ceiling and the light diffusers at the window.

OPPOSITE RIGHT

Wall bench detail

1 Heavy duty Velcro
2 Plastic hard backing
3 Recycled polymer fabric
4 Steel tube frame
5 Translucent fabric
6 Solid wood
7 LED rope light
8 Timber blocking
9 Plyboo flooring sheet
10 Plywood
11 Sheetrock
12 Weld
13 Steel tube
14 Upholstery
15 Upholstery foam
16 Plyboo subflooring

THIS PAGE

Folded and twisted recycled stainless steel troughs mimic the pattern of the Plyboo and conceal LED light sources.

LEFT
Sloping Plyboo cladding for columns and walls provides ergonomically efficient leaning posts and conceals uplighters. The veneer finish of the plywood chairs bridges the gap between the Plyboo pattern and white tabletops.

OPPOSITE TOP LEFT
Cantilevered trays carry cups and tubs at leaning posts.

OPPOSITE BOTTOM LEFT
Plan of cantilevered shelf.

OPPOSITE RIGHT
Leaning wall detail
1 Translucent fabric on steel tube frame
2 Solid wood
3 Plyboo flooring
4 Plywood
5 Folded steel table
6 Steel plate
7 Bolt
8 Timber blocking

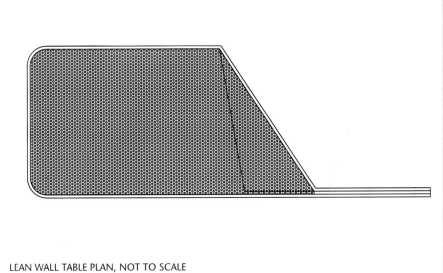

LEAN WALL TABLE PLAN, NOT TO SCALE

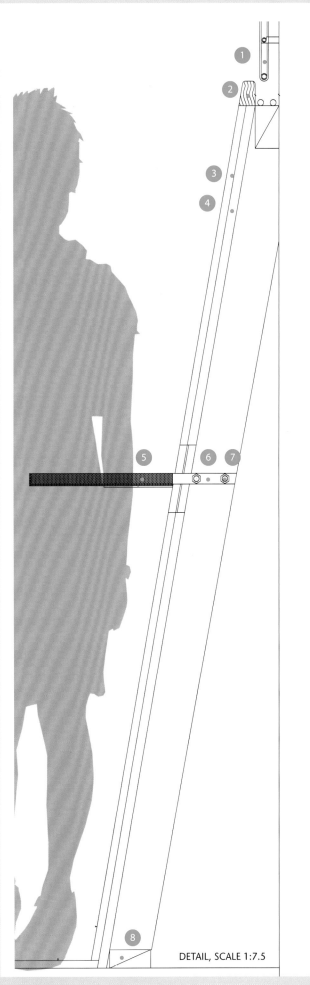

DETAIL, SCALE 1:7.5

YELLOW SUBMARINE, MUNICH
TULP

When dealing with an awkward space, it is generally considered wise to make a virtue of its shortcomings. If a physical restriction cannot be eliminated, it is more productive to see it as a stimulus that can prompt the imagination to explore unfamiliar territory. The development of this cafe, for the staff of an advertising agency, saw a windowless basement evolve from subterranean to submarine.

The restricted area of the original room ensured that the hard-edged geometry and tight planning of the new installation were closer to the reality of space in an operational submarine than the whimsy implied by the 'Yellow Submarine' sobriquet. Rather than attempt a perceptual extension of the original room's boundaries the designers chose to reduce it further, to create a room within a room that is uncompromised by the existing structural piers, ceiling beams and irregularities of plan that had destroyed the coherence of an earlier version of the cafe. Now the zone between new clean and irregular existing walls is used for storage and service distribution.

To express the independence of the new from the old, all existing exposed elements are painted charcoal grey, as a neutral backdrop for the yellow-stained, spruce-veneered plywood sheets that are used for all new wall, floor, ceiling and furniture elements. The skewed plan is established by the angle at which the stairs from above meet the floor, and the strictly right-angled junctions of horizontal and vertical faces underline the distortions on plan. The single table and bench seating encourage social interaction and the hard surfaces, which are acceptable for the duration of a lunch break, offer relief from the upholstered cosseting of anthropometric office furniture.

A white-painted column is the only existing element to intrude into the new installation and it is incorporated as a support for the cantilevered kitchen counter, the open end of which is cut to match the angle of the junction of the two floor finishes. Frameless panels of backlit turquoise glass in the walls and ceiling suggest the water in which the 'Yellow Submarine' metaphorically floats.

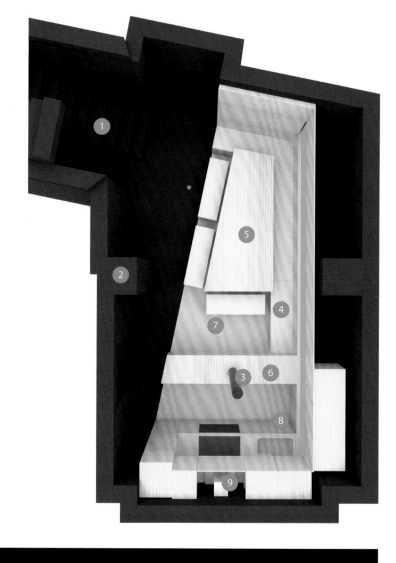

TOP
Model from above: the angle of the stair establishes the angle of the new floor.
1 Stair access
2 Existing walls
3 Existing column
4 Bench seating
5 Table
6 Counter
7 Kitchen
8 Services
9 Storage

BOTTOM
As staff descend the stairs the new installation 'floats' in the charcoal grey of the existing elements.

TOP

The squared corners of the benches contrast with the angles of the plan. The existing column supports the cantilevered counter, the open end of which is cut to match the angle of floor finishes.

BOTTOM

Lengths of counter top meet at and are cut around the existing column. The vertical divider is offset to miss the column. Junctions of plywood and glass are aligned.

GREY GOOSE BAR, BRUSSELS
PURESANG

This bar, for a vodka distilling company, fulfils two roles. It provides a social environment that complements the brand image and incorporates a slightly more formal area for business discussions.

The perimeter of the original rectilinear space is lined with mirror, traditionally and frequently used in bars to extend and dramatize dimensions. However, rather than installing a flat mirror that predictably replicates the image of the original, the designers have dressed the wall behind the bar/table with a skin of triangular blue-tinted mirrors, mounted on an angled structure built out from the existing wall surface, which offer a fragmented image of the interior and the, otherwise unspectacular, cityscape beyond its windows.

A significantly more spectacular city of leaning towers is suggested by the distorted reflection of the regular geometries of the backlit floor to ceiling shelves, which block an existing window, and the 126 identical bottles they carry. The long shelf set into the mirrored wall behind the bar, which contains a regularly spaced, bottom-lit, row of bottles that are reflected in the blue mirror on the back of the recess, adds to the uncertain boundaries between real and reflected elements.

The bar countertop and table are expressed as a continuous element, connected visually at floor level, and the angled horizontal and vertical gloss white planes make physical the distortions presented in the mirrored wall behind it. These are also echoed more modestly by the wall bench at the entrance. Bar and table were constructed as a single element on-site, to ensure perfect alignments along their length and with existing elements. The lighting structure that hangs above and follows the line of bar and table is custom-made and intended to suggest sparkling ice. Its reflection in the mirrored wall, bar top and table provides another ambiguous plane. The skeletal configuration of the chairs at the meeting table conform to the triangularity of the mirror facets while the solid masses of the bar stools float appropriately in the mirrored front of the bar counter.

RIGHT
Angled planes, multiplied and reflected in fragmented mirrors and gloss finishes, deconstruct the original rectangular space. The orderly lines of bottles, real and reflected, in the recessed shelf contrast with the mirrored distortion of the window. The reflected blocks of the bar stools float in the mirrored front of the bar counter. The bespoke light fitting follows the line of bar and table.

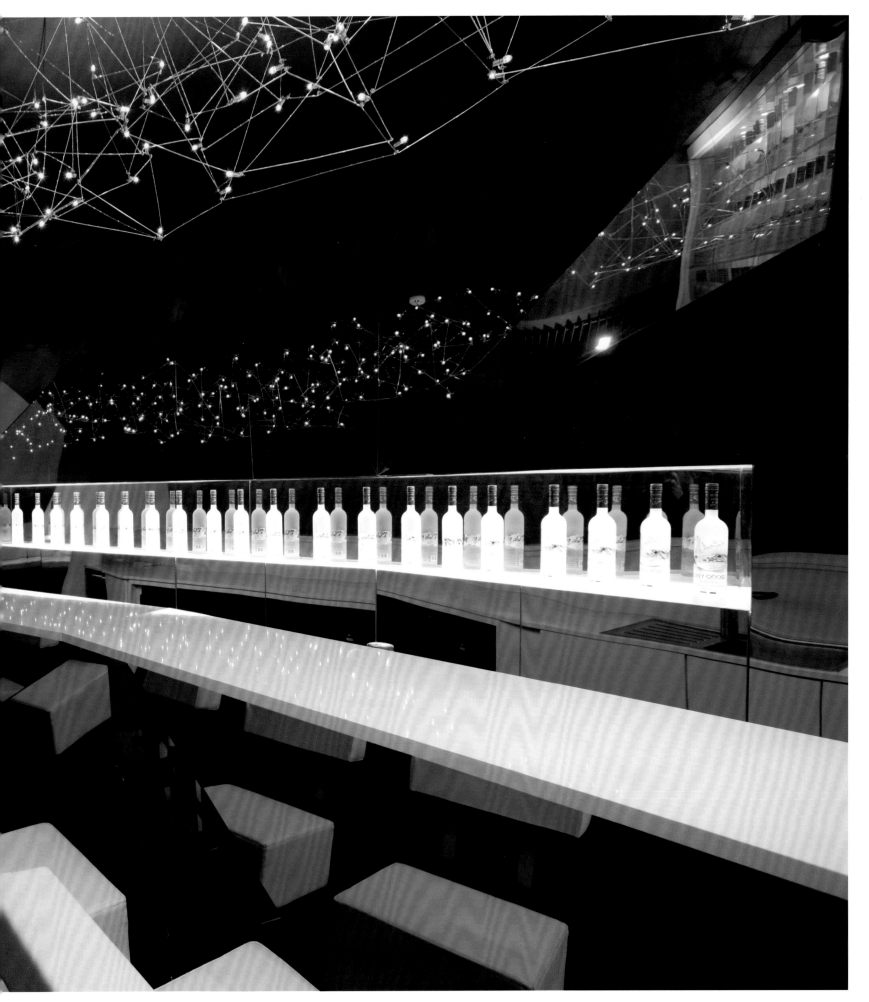

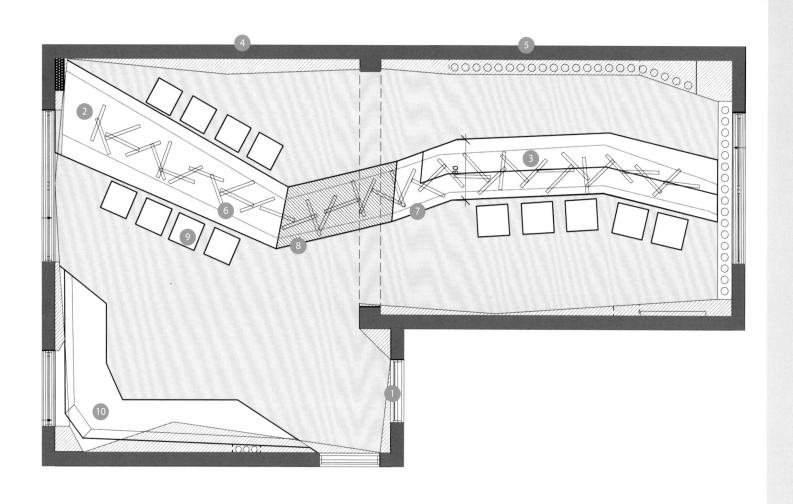

PLAN, SCALE 1:50

RIGHT

A continuous horizontal and vertical central rib braces the white gloss MDF top and end panel of the table. The triangulated structure of the chair relates to the shape of the wall mirrors and the fragmented image within them. The footprint of the table/bar strip at floor level further distorts perspective.

OPPOSITE LEFT

Plan

1 Entrance
2 Meeting table
3 Bar counter
4 Mirrored wall
5 Recessed bottle shelf
6 Light fitting
7 Backlit display shelves
8 Floor level strip
9 Stools
10 Bench

OPPOSITE BOTTOM LEFT

The reflection of the backlit display wall is distorted in the wall mirror to suggest an expressionistic cityscape reminiscent of the reflected view through the window at the other end of the room.

BOTTOM MIDDLE

Mirrors are glued to a plywood base on a timber frame.

BOTTOM RIGHT

The table/bar counter was constructed on site to ensure precise junctions with exiting elements.

RESTAURANTS

BANGALORE EXPRESS WATERLOO, LONDON
OUTLINE

The decorative elements of this restaurant, which serves Indian fast food, relate to the pace of the busy, noisy street outside but the tiered booths of its reworked plan and section provide customers with a degree of privacy. In anticipation of the possibility of creating a small chain of similar outlets, all elements are designed to be realizable in a range of locations.

On this pioneering site the original space was stripped back to the three separate areas created by the existing structural walls of the original shell. The subdivision provides intimacy and intelligent planning creates views through and between the zones to make a cohesive whole. The kitchen is open to the eating areas, to provide a little drama and demonstrate efficiency.

The materials and techniques used to construct what initially appears to be a complex solution are simple and cheap. The 2.4m x 1.2m (8 x 4 ft) fire-retardant MDF wall cladding panels were fixed temporarily to plasterboard base partitions, the patterns were marked out in situ, the panels were removed and 6mm (¼ in) deep grooves were cut by circular saw. The panels were then refixed and redecorated. The MDF cladding eliminates the need for skirting boards. The grooves and some of the triangular areas are painted dark grey, others a lighter grey, but the majority are a muted green. Together they make for a calmer environment. The fragmented planes and colour masses erode the bulk of walls that define what is a comparatively tight space.

A line of double-height four-person booths runs the length of one side of the restaurant. Each of the upper units, which together provide twenty-four extra seats, is accessed by a stepladder and is assembled from proprietary scaffolding components. A mock-up of both levels was made before final installation to test and evolve the practicality of the structure, for both customers and staff. The lower units have restricted head height, which is acceptable because customers slide sideways into booths in a semi-seated position. The same scaffolding system also supports the two-person benches that line the long communal tables. The tabletops are all walnut-veneered 40mm (1½ in) thick blockboard and the benches are phenolic coated birch plywood with dark brown stained cut edges.

RIGHT
Lowered ceiling panels accommodate recessed lights and air conditioning equipment.

Caution

Caution

LEFT
Ladders provide support for the tables at floor level. Small notices advise caution.

RIGHT & FAR RIGHT
Sections through booths
1 Existing ceiling
2 Division/support walls
3 Cladding to existing wall
4 Fixing collar
5 'Scaffolding' handrail
6 'Scaffolding' table support
7 Veneered plywood panel
8 Timber-block bench seat
9 Softwood framing
10 Sheet flooring
11 Softwood floor joists supported on dividing walls
12 'Scaffolding' ladder
13 General floor level
14 Tabletop

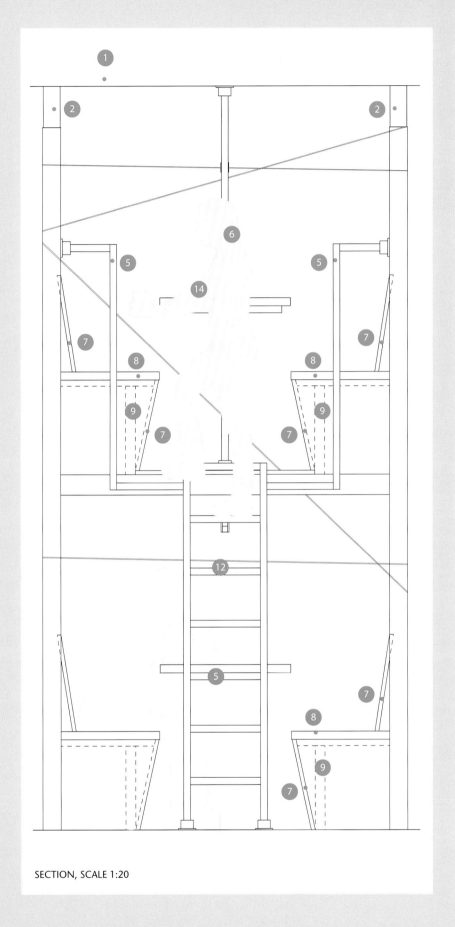

SECTION, SCALE 1:20

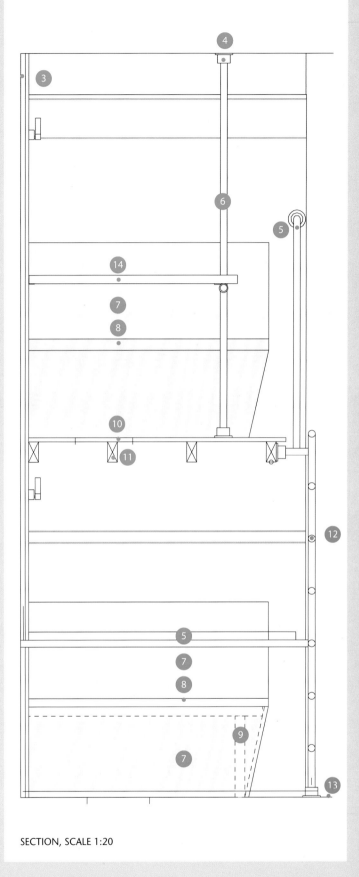

SECTION, SCALE 1:20

ABOVE
Cantilevered edge rails provide security on the upper level and support for customers and staff using the ladder.

LEFT TOP
Elevation of booths
1 Existing structure
2 'Scaffolding' structure
3 Dividing/supporting wall
4 'Scaffolding' handrail
5 Table
6 Bench
7 Ladder

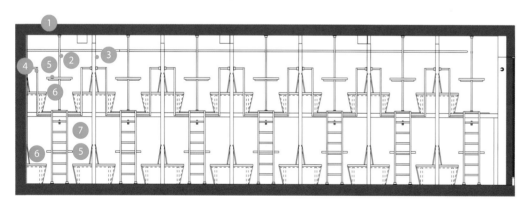

ELEVATION, SCALE 1:100

LEFT BOTTOM
Plan of booths
1 Existing wall
2 Void
3 Bench
4 Table
5 Ladder

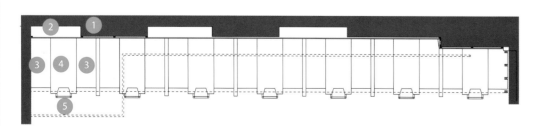

PLAN, SCALE 1:100

ABOVE
Angled patterns break up flat wall surfaces and imply mass and solidity at corners.

RIGHT
Two levels of booths, accessed by ladders, are assembled from proprietary scaffolding components that also provide support for the central tables and the bench seating.

BANGALORE EXPRESS CITY, LONDON
OUTLINE

The location for the second restaurant in the Bangalore Express chain offers a very different context. This occupies a much larger space in a more substantial building on a corner site in London's financial district, and caters for a less casual, probably more affluent, clientele. Detailing responds to these changes. The reception and bar area are at ground level with the restaurant, kitchen and other services on the significantly larger basement level. While the irregularly shaped upper level has street views, the basement has no natural light and, as in the prototype, is divided into more intimate spaces arranged around a central spine booths, which are further consolidated by a lowered ceiling of the same veneer.

The decorative motifs used on the ground floor walls anticipate those in the basement and the solid balustrade around the stairwell connects the two. The principle of angular subdivision of wall surfaces, introduced in the first restaurant is adopted and amended. Materials and fabrication techniques are the same but colours are more assertive. The dominant reds conform to a more conventional perception of an 'Indian' colour palette. The grooves that divide the blocks of colour are painted in the brighter of the two reds and continue through the darker colours.

The lack of natural light in the basement also allows, and requires in compensation for the lack of views, a more complex lighting solution. The coffering of ceiling planes, inspired by those in the traditional banking halls of the district, creates vertical surfaces that either catch light from concealed sources or make deep shadows. Together they dematerialize the ceiling plane and suggest greater height. Sleeved LED strip lights, set in a tray below the bar countertop of acid-etched glass backed with opal diffuser film to increase its translucency, are reflected in the mirrored soffit of the bar gantry.

TOP
The walls of the stairwell make a link between ground-floor reception and the bar and the basement restaurant spaces. Coloured bands wrap around the central wall and tonal changes emphasize three-dimensionality.

RIGHT
Plan: basement
1 Entrance
2 Main booths
3 Small booths
4 Dining room
5 Banquette seating
6 Fire escape stair

PLAN, SCALE 1:200

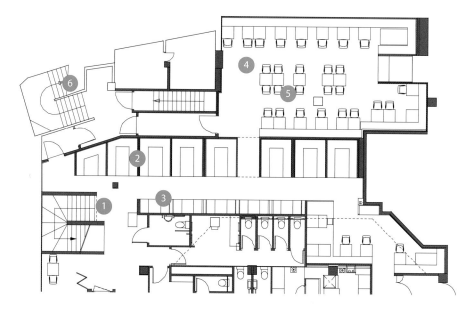

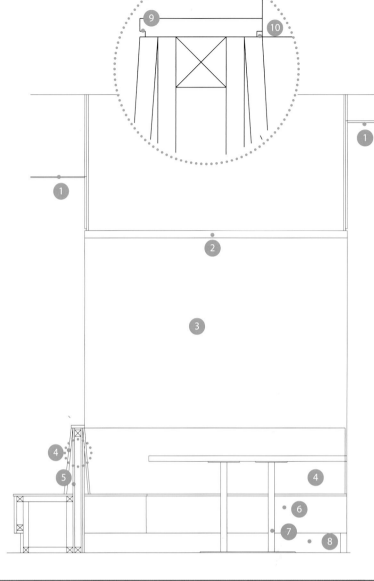

TOP LEFT

Lights behind the translucent glass bar top are reflected in the mirrored base of the gantry overhead.

TOP RIGHT

Section

1 Plasterboard ceiling
2 Cavity for service elements
3 Walnut-veneered MDF sides and ceiling
4 18mm (¾ in) painted plywood back panel
5 70 x 70mm (2¾ x 2¾ in) softwood framing
6 Walnut-veneered base panel
7 Stainless steel tubular base to 40mm (1½ in) walnut top
8 Painted timber plinth
9 Seating back finished flush with top piece. 6mm (¼ in) shadow gap
10 Gap plugged in line with the dividing partition

RIGHT

Front elevation of booth

1 Painted 12mm (½ in) shadow gap between plasterboard and veneered MDF
2 Walnut-veneered ceiling sides and front
3 Painted 18mm (¾ in) MDF with 6mm (¼ in) grooves cut to define pattern
4 Painted plywood back and seat
5 40mm (1½ in) walnut table top on brushed stainless steel base
6 Walnut-veneered MDF base panel
7 Painted timber plinth

SECTION, SCALE 1:25

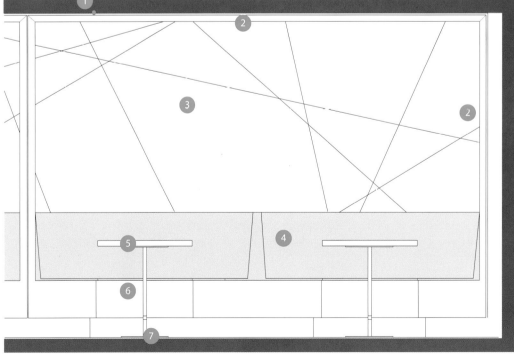

ELEVATION, SCALE 1:25

LEFT
Booths give structure to the central area. Cantilevered tables for two are paired between vertically extended backrests to subdivide the room further. Larger tables are grouped under a lowered ceiling.

MIDDLE
Elevation of booths
1 Painted 18mm (¾ in) fire-retardant MDF with 6mm (¼ in) wide grooves
2 Painted back and seat to bench
3 40mm (1½ in) walnut tabletop on stainless steel base
4 Walnut-veneered panel to bench front
5 Painted timber plinth
6 Higher plasterboard ceiling over circulation zone
7 Aluminium ventilation grill
8 Walnut-veneered ceiling over booth

BOTTOM
Plan of main booths
1 Bench seat
2 Table
3 Dividing partition
4 Wall clad in 18mm (¾ in) fire-retardant MDF with 6mm (¼ in) wide grooves.
5 Corridor to dining room

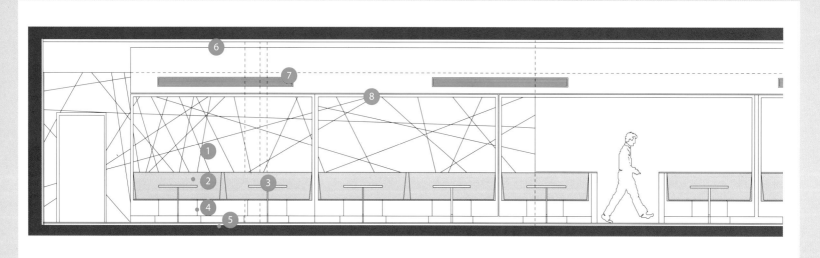

ELEVATION, SCALE 1:100

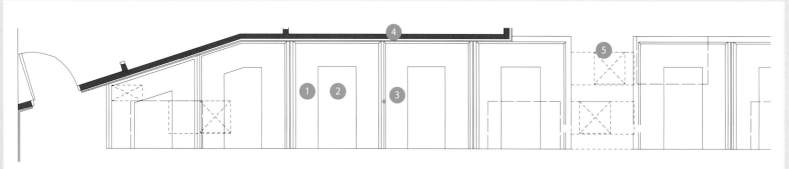

PLAN, SCALE 1:100

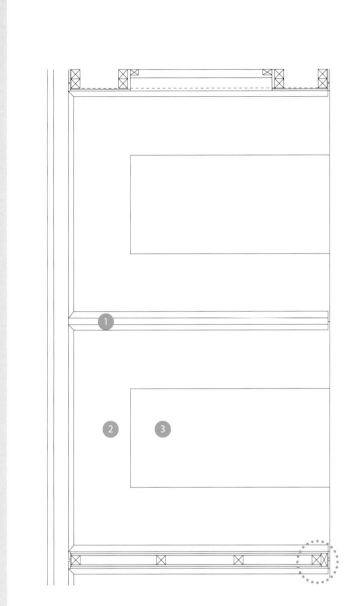

ELEVATION, SCALE 1:25

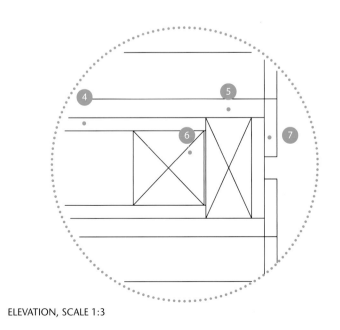

ELEVATION, SCALE 1:3

LEFT
Detail plan of booth
1 Dividing partition
2 Bench
3 Table
4 12mm (½ in) structural plywood sheet
5 18mm (¾ in) walnut-veneered MDF cladding panel
6 70 x 70mm (2¾ x 2¾ in) softwood stud framing
7 18mm (¾ in) walnut-veneered MDF front piece

ABOVE
Grooves cut into the wall board are painted in a brighter red.

BEIJING NOODLE NO.9, LAS VEGAS
DESIGN SPIRITS

This casual dining area in one of Las Vegas' major casinos has been detailed to create an immersive visual experience that is intense enough to coexist with the steady flow of background noise filtering through from the adjacent gaming areas. The room is entered between lines of ceiling-high tanks in which elaborately finned red Ryukin fish make kinetic patterns that anticipate the density and intensity of the static patterns within the room itself.

Complex small-scale arabesque patterns, derived from leaf and frond forms, blur the boundaries between walls, ceiling, floor and furniture. Each is achieved with methods and materials appropriate to their particular location and function. Applied patterning is layered to increase its complexity. Silver patterns were created using Illustrator software and cut digitally from carbon fibre vinyl film and applied to a matt white painted base coat on 9mm (⅜ in) plasterboard walls and ceiling suggesting additional shadows cast by the perforated pattern laser-cut into the suspended 1.5m (5 ft) square and 5mm (³⁄₁₆ in) thick steel panels. This pattern is similar but calculatedly different both in form and size. LED light sources behind the panels illuminate the silver patterns and cast shadows on the floor and furniture. The high-level dividing screens are sheets of white powder-coated steel,1.5m (5 ft) square and 5mm (³⁄₁₆ in), with laser-cut perforated motifs.

The off-white tones of furniture and floor maximize the effect of shadows and the white varnished ash tabletops have white painted leaf patterns, protected by clear varnish. Further shadow patterns are cast on to the ash floor, which is finished with a white varnish and a urethane seal. All fronts to the counter and service stations, low dividing walls and bases of the fish tanks carry the universal pattern, which is repeated with self-adhesive plastic decals mounted on the back of the 10mm (⅜ in) glass counter top and the 12mm (½ in) glass counter front, which sits proud of a silver pattern stencilled onto matt white 9mm (⅜ in) plasterboard.

ABOVE RIGHT
The room is entered between rows of fish tanks. The layered ceiling extends into the dining area. The ubiquitous pattern is stencilled on vertical surfaces and applied as decals to glass surfaces.

RIGHT
The silver vinyl film ceiling pattern is visible through the suspended perforated steel sheet. The rear wall is lined with jars containing colour-coordinated beans.

ABOVE
The single layer of the perforated 5mm
(³⁄₁₆ in) steel screen is supported by the
back of banquette seating and ceiling.

RIGHT
The heads of perforated partitions are
fixed, with angled cleats, to the 5mm
(³⁄₁₆ in) steel ceiling panels.

PIZZA PEREZ, SYRACUSE
FRANCESCO MONCADA

Difficulties demand an ingenious reconsideration of strategies, and the best interiors are often the result of a designer having to deal with restrictions, sometimes physical, very frequently financial. This example demonstrates the potential of using comparatively cheap materials, particularly if they are also simple to assemble and so reduce labour costs.

A wide new wall divides the restaurant into two areas, one a bar and counter for takeaway orders, the other for eating in. It wraps up an existing central column and has several functions; displaying wine and menu ingredients, storing customers' coats and baggage and concealing air conditioning and audio equipment. The wall and ceiling are clad in unrefined fibreglass sheets that are more normally used in industrial or agricultural construction. Those on the ceiling are corrugated to add rigidity; those on the wall are flat. Both are screwed to timber framing, which is visible through the semitransparent sheets. Straight lengths of neon tube light the takeaway. Less familiar circular tubes light the restaurant and suggest an upgrade.

Marine plywood sheets clad the floor and the wall to the kitchen, where they are fixed to timber battens screwed to an existing wall. The stainless-steel countertop rests on stacked metal boxes that are painted white and provide both a rigid base and storage compartments. All surfaces in the lavatories are finished with waterproof paint. Two finely executed graphic pieces, created in collaboration with Point Supreme, decorate the white-painted side walls and do much, comparatively cheaply, to counteract any impression of frugality. The zebra in the entrance area is a conundrum to encourage speculation and conversation. In the restaurant area a quasi-scientific matrix diagram sets out the variety of possible ingredients and the complexity of the combinations that may be generated from them in a decorative device that finally introduces a little applied colour.

TOP
The view from the street is dominated by the corrugated fibreglass ceiling and the graphic devices on the side walls.

RIGHT
Plan
1 Entrance
2 Zebra wall
3 Storage/display wall
4 Matrix wall
5 Takeaway counter
6 Kitchen
7 Service hatch
8 WCs

OPPOSITE
A timber-framed, fibreglass-clad wall wraps up an existing column, providing storage and an open display slot that connects the bar and takeaway with the restaurant.

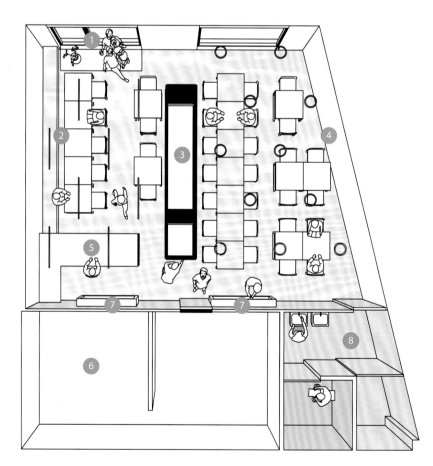

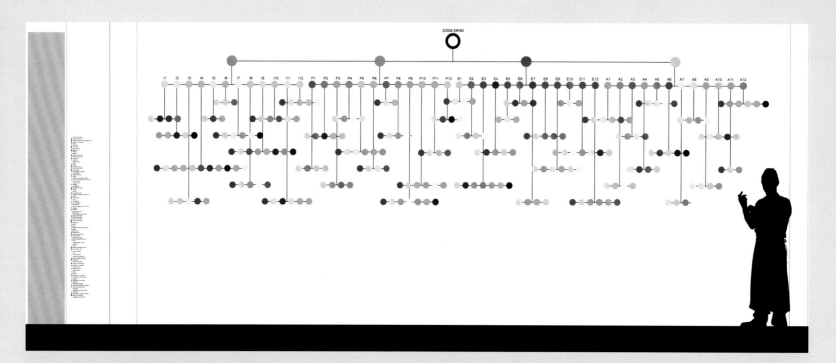

TOP

The matrix diagram, setting out ingredients and combinations of ingredients, introduces colour in the restaurant in contrast to the zebra.

LEFT

Circular neon lights and the coloured dots of the matrix diagram represent a modest upgrading of elements in the restaurant. The central wall protects the tightly packed tables from the informality of the takeaway.

OPPOSITE TOP

The framing and screws fixing the fibreglass sheets to the wall and ceiling are clearly visible. The black stripes of the zebra are isolated on the white wall, as are the dots of the matrix in the restaurant.

OPPOSITE BOTTOM LEFT

Waterproof paint replaces more expensive finishes in the lavatory areas and, apart from the matrix diagram and occasional table legs in the restaurant, provides the only bright colour.

OPPOSITE BOTTOM RIGHT

Floor and kitchen walls are marine plywood. The countertop, which rests on stacked white metal boxes, is stainless steel.

TOAST, NAVATO
STANLEY SAITOWITZ/ NATOMA ARCHITECTS

Toast serves comfort food for breakfast, lunch and dinner and this, in a mall north of San Francisco, is its second branch. Entering its 12m (39 ft) high volume has been compared to walking into a loaf of bread, with the unpainted particleboard wall cladding and its apparently randomly shaped holes having some of the colour and visual texture of bread. Upgrading the status of this mundane building material to that of decorative cladding and its near universal application, which is augmented by chair and table laminates that are close to it in tone and texture, produces a visual coherence that, with the atrium of the original shell, gives the new interior something approaching monumentality.

The 19mm (¾ in) particleboard, finished with a clear, water-based sealant and fixed to a timber subframe with concealed 'Z' clips, clads external wall areas, the partitions that separate public and service areas, the bar with its hanging cube and the lowered ceiling over the entrance. All vertical surfaces are perforated. CNC technology ensures precision in cutting individual holes and allows variation in their distribution so that the absence of repeat pattern reduces the perception of individual boards. Holes in counter fronts and counters are closed by backing sheets on their inside faces.

Construction techniques adhere to the logic of the boards' standard dimensions and structural capabilities. Generally there is no attempt to conceal the simple directness of the fabrication. While the cube over the bar presents smooth surfaces, with apparently deep recesses, to the greater space, its framed construction is exposed on the inner faces and the recesses revealed to be no more than cantilevered linings to the openings.

Other display and storage recesses are separated by the thickness of the single board that supports them. Shelves, cantilevered to carry wine bottles, are the thickness of the board. Only where function or appearance demands extra depth, as for the waiter station at the bar, are mitred joints used to provide an unbroken continuation of the perforated surface and to avoid exposing the boards' rougher core.

ABOVE
The particleboard, perforated with the cut-out shapes, which are also incorporated into the logo, defines the interior. The bar faces the entrance and an open kitchen is to the left.

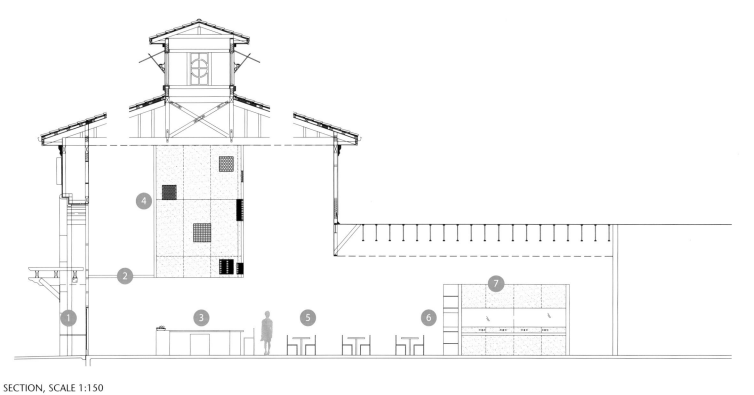

SECTION, SCALE 1:150

TOP LEFT

Framing is exposed on the inside of the cube above the bar. What appeared to be deep recesses in a solid wall on the exterior are revealed to be boxes cantilevered off the outer skin.

TOP RIGHT

Vertical and horizontal sheets are slotted together to make the display and storage unit on the right. The necessary projection of the horizontals on the outer edge makes a narrow display shelf.

BOTTOM

Section
1 Entrance
2 Lowered ceiling
3 Bar
4 Suspended 'tower'

5 Communal tables
6 Slotted storage wall
7 WCs

TOP
Particleboard is turned down, with a mitred joint, on the edges of the bar and the waiter station to avoid exposing the rougher core of the board.

BOTTOM LEFT & RIGHT
CNC makes large and small holes with equal precision. The colour and visual texture of the tables and chairs is close to the finish of the particleboard and gives it credibility as a finishing material.

CAVE, SYDNEY
KOICHI TAKADA

A persistent complaint about restaurant interiors is that noise levels are unpleasantly high, undermining the pleasure of the social experience. The problem is exacerbated as diners increase their individual volumes in response to, but further contributing to, the general escalation. The interior of this Japanese restaurant was shaped, literally, by an ambition to create a comfortable auditory experience for individual groups of diners within the communal environment.

Secondary structures were added to wall and ceiling surfaces to eliminate the smooth parallel surfaces that reflect and amplify sound waves. They are expressed as a succession of plywood ribs at 150mm (6 in) intervals and these further break up surface planes and reduce reflection. The vault forms, whose scale and profile makes them the dominant visual element within the interior, and their configuration responds to the floor plan, sweeping low over the central sushi service track and high above customer zones.

Computer-modelling techniques were used to test and develop profiles and the final data was transferred to Computer Numerical Control (CNC) equipment, in order to maximize the number of ribs that could be cut from standard 1.2 x 2.4m (4 x 8 ft) sheets of 16mm (⅝ in) thick, Marenti veneered plywood. The veneered components that make up each rib were assembled on-site, with glued biscuit joints to ensure precise alignment of each face. Ribs were stained before, and touched up after, installation.

Ribs are each fixed to a timber strip at floor level. Painted plywood infill panels conceal low-level wall fixings, cause the ribs to taper visually at floor level and conceal uplighters in customer areas. In the service kitchen the painted panels sit in front of the ribs to eliminate dirt-collecting projections, and overhead lighting is bright and evenly spread. Over customer seating light levels are lower, from long cylindrical stainless steel downlighters that occasionally hang between ribs. A timber ramp, which matches the Tasmanian Oak floor finish, and the black blocks of single steps give customers access to the raised sitting zones. The change of height allows them to engage at eye level with staff who stand behind the service counter.

ABOVE
The smooth plywood ribs dip over the sushi conveyor belt.

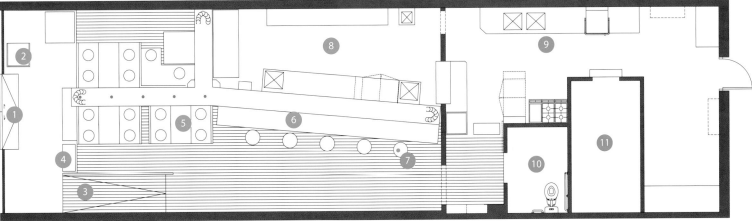

PLAN, SCALE 1:100

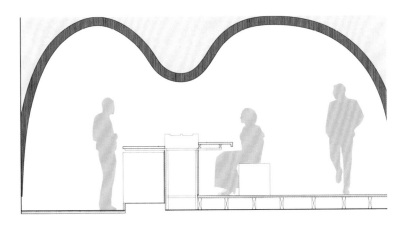

TOP

The profile of the plywood ribs is revealed through the glazed street elevation and the areas within the restaurant are clearly defined. The ramp and black steps lead to the raised levels. Light is concentrated over the open kitchen.

BOTTOM

The ribs mask irregularities in the existing ceiling. The raised floor gives customers and kitchen staff a shared eye level.

MIDDLE

Plan
1 Entrance
2 Reception
3 Ramp
4 Steps
5 Table
6 Bench seat
7 Stool
8 Service kitchen
9 Preparation kitchen
10 WC
11 Store

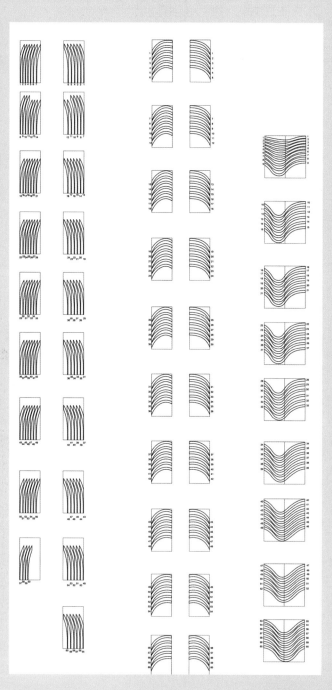

TOP LEFT
CNC cutting facilitated maximum use of
1.2 x 2.4m (4 x 8 ft) plywood sheets.

TOP RIGHT
Ribs were pre-fabricated off-site.

BOTTOM RIGHT
CNC production ensured compatibility
of abutting elements cut from different
sheets.

Sections were installed in order and joints were glued and clamped while drying. The white inserts between ribs conceal light sources.

BOTTOM
Variations in veneer pattern indicate joints.

TREE, SYDNEY
KOICHI TAKADA

This project has clear similarities with the slightly earlier Cave project (page 134) by the same designers for the same client, and offers another example of how a brand identity can be sustained without literal reiteration of every element (also see Bangalore Express Waterloo and Bangalore Express City, pages 114 and 120). The reference to and interpretation of a natural phenomenon remains but the expression is here shaped by the irregular geometry of the plan. As in Cave, a ramp leads to a raised floor area, which ensures a single level for the sushi conveyor belt serving customers seated at conventional benches and high-level stools and gives both a shared eye-level with staff in the central open kitchen. Rather than the vertical sweep of ribs in Cave, here they extend horizontally and at a constant height from the radiused vertical 'trunk' pieces that conceal an existing structural column.

The horizontal 'branches', their individuality emphasized by the black-painted ceiling behind them, extend until they almost touch the perimeter walls and the variation in their lengths makes an asymmetrical structure that suggests a natural form as readily as it does a geometric one. The space between 'branches' opens up towards the real trees beyond the windows but they also create a darker, more enclosed space at the back where a thickly encrusted plaster finish on the solid perimeter walls, its texture amplified by wall-mounted uplighters, suggests another natural phenomenon.

The plywood elements here were cut using conventional tools and techniques rather than CNC. It was decided that this would be as effective because the rib shapes are simpler, with each curved vertical sharing the same profile. Ribs were pre-fabricated off-site but various fixing details, appropriate to local conditions, were agreed by the designer and contractor on-site. Connections of rib components are glued biscuit joints and staining was touched up after installation.

Irregularly spaced lights, which loosely follow the line of the sushi conveyor belt are set back between the plywood ribs and create an irregular – organic – pattern. Table and countertops in the public areas are black-stained Tasmanian Oak, equipment in the kitchen is stainless steel. The floor is commercial grade ceramic tiles and a small cushion-lined pen is provided for children.

TOP
Plywood ribs encircle the existing structural column in the middle of the open kitchen and spread across the ceiling, stopping just short of the windows.

BOTTOM
Fixed tables and benches occupy the upper level with the children's area just behind.

TOP LEFT
Simple geometric forms and patterns are complicated by foreshortened and angled views.

TOP RIGHT
At the rear the ribs stop short of the textured plaster wall. A high-level counter is served by the sushi conveyor.

BELOW
Plan
1 Entrance
2 Vertical ribs ('trunk') around the existing column
3 Ceiling ribs ('branches')
4 Waiting
5 Ramp
6 Fixed tables and seating
7 High-level counter with stools
8 Sushi conveyor
9 Kitchen
10 Children's area
11 Wash-up and storage
12 WCs
13 Office

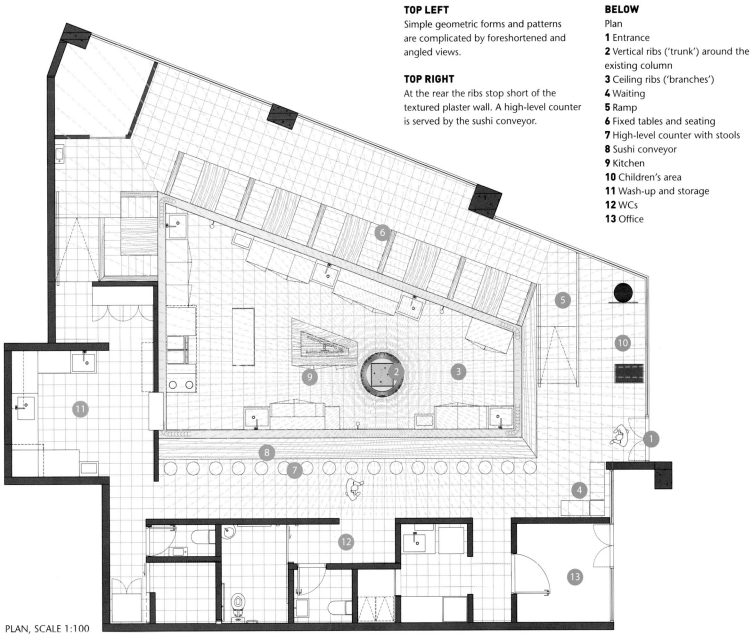

PLAN, SCALE 1:100

THAI RESTAURANT, LJUBLJANA
ELASTIK ARCHITECTURE

This self-service restaurant is located in Ljubljana's biggest shopping mall. It had an appropriately modest budget for its upgrading but the designers had no inclination to make extravagant gestures or expensively literal references to Thai culture. They concentrated instead on maximizing the impact of the ceiling, the area immune to the wear of high customer traffic, to provide identity and character. While aspects of the detailing, particularly the capitals to the columns, are not precisely in the Thai tradition they are strange enough to Western eyes to suggest something Eastern.

The ceiling is composed of ribs cut, using CNC technology, from sheets of untreated white poplar-veneered plywood. The ribs were cut short on-site to maintain an even gap at the perimeter and are suspended on rods fixed to the soffit of the structural floor slab above. They conceal lighting, air conditioning ductwork and drainage from the kitchen on the next level. Individual ribs may be removed for maintenance access. The two ribs that hang lowest abut the existing columns but leave a small gap between edge of rib and column to allow for unevenness in the faces of the columns. Regular spacing and a consistent relationship to the column is maintained by a length of timber, fixed to the column, between the pair and to which each is connected by dowels.

Control of the levels, location and colour of lighting allows variations in ambience and enhances the three-dimensionality of the column 'capitals'. The light coloured ribs are complemented by the black floor finish and the wenge laminate, a dark wood with a strong reddish grain pattern, which is used for tables and the booth seating.

TOP
Light is concentrated to suggest column capitals. The black metal suspension rods are visible between the ribs.

RIGHT
Plan
1 Entrance
2 New 'Thai' Columns
3 Self-service counters
4 Existing columns

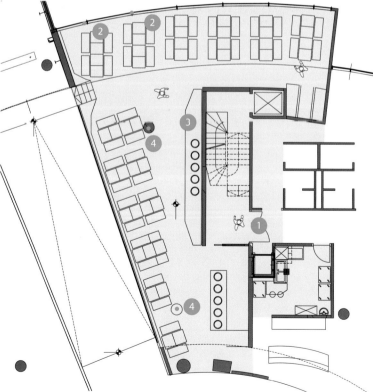

PLAN, SCALE 1:200

RIGHT
Individual ribs are hung close enough to suggest a solid, undulating ceiling plane. Column 'capitals' are unfamiliar enough to suggest the Orient.

BOTTOM LEFT
Ribs meeting the columns are screwed to timber blocks that are, in turn, screwed to the column to ensure even alignment.

BOTTOM RIGHT
CNC production facilitates the production of a range of consistent profiles.

CONDUIT, SAN FRANCISCO
STANLEY SAITOWITZ/ NATOMA ARCHITECTS

The height of the comparatively large floor area of this ground-floor restaurant is restricted by the floor slab of the residential accommodation above it and, while a suspended ceiling would conceal the random collection of plumbing, electrical and sprinkler conduits serving the upper floors, it would also exacerbate the perception of restricted ceiling height.

The solution, and consequently the restaurant's name, were suggested by the existing service pipes and the insertion of new vertical layers of high-gloss pipes, fixed to floor and ceiling by proprietary channels, assimilates and masks their arbitrary distribution. Existing pipes and other service elements are painted black to reduce their visibility further. Vertical divisions, of new galvanized and copper lengths, subdivide the expanse of floor and punctuate the table layout. The area given over to free-standing tables is further defined by a carpet that contrasts with the black granite tiles of the perimeter circulation spaces.

The table area is shielded from the entrance by two vertical batteries of pipes, one galvanized, one copper, and by a black metal fire box and flue that serves as a supersized conduit. The fronts of a dining bench, with views to the open kitchen and the bar, are clad with horizontal lines of galvanized and copper pipes. Screens of vertical pipes divide banquette positions.

Detailing of joints and junctions is appropriately refined. Short lengths of tubes are slid within abutting lengths to provide rigid bridging and alignment and are tightened in position with 'allen key' joints. The lining through of joints brings visible order to the installation. A canopy of copper pipes establishes the conduit motif over the entrance. Hanging copper letters spell out the name and the red wooden doors harmonize with the metal.

TOP
The canopy of copper pipes signals the principal elements of the interior. The circle on the central column provides an exit for the flue.

MIDDLE
Screens of vertical pipes and a black fire box and flue provide barriers between tables and the entrance. The tables sit on a carpet and black granite tiles mark the circulation areas.

BOTTOM
Copper pipes divide banquette positions. The presence of functioning wall-mounted service pipes is lessened by the cosmetic additions.

TOP
Horizontal crisscrossing layers of
galvanized pipes visually shield the black-
painted existing ceiling-mounted service
elements. Horizontal rows of galvanized
and copper pipes clad the fronts of bar
and dining bench.

RIGHT
Plan
1 Entrance
2 Fire box
3 Dining
4 Bar
5 Dining counter
6 Kitchen
7 Vertical pipework screens

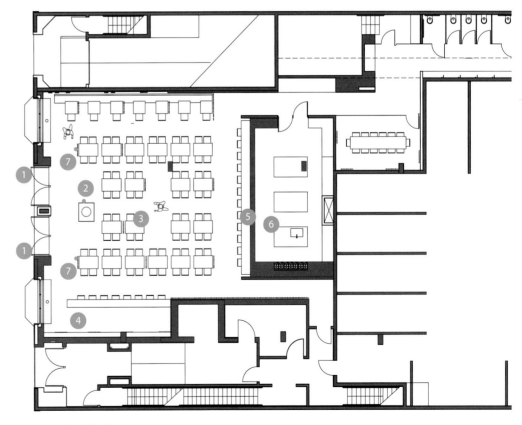

PLAN, SCALE 1:200

NISEKO LOOKOUT CAFÉ, HOKKAIDO
DESIGN SPIRITS

Commercial clients invariably want their interiors completed quickly, so that trading may begin and profits may be made. Time restrictions for the completion of this mountain-top cafe were even more demanding than usual, with the designer appointed in early October and a projected completion date set for mid-November, in time for the four or five month ski season. The site presented further problems of access for materials, machinery and workers. Rain prohibited access because of the danger of landslides and the short winter hours of daylight further restricted work. A warm winter and a late snowfall did however extend the construction period until late November. With a projected 45 days between commission and completion the design was conceived in four days and approved on the fifth. To speed construction the range of materials was restricted to timber, paint and wallpaper, all of which were easy to transport up the mountain and quick to assemble and apply on site.

Japanese visitors represent less than 10 percent of customer numbers and the planes, of 20mm x 35mm ($^{13}/_{16}$ x $1^{3}/_{8}$ in) spruce-timber strips at 150mm (6 in) intervals, were chosen to conform to overseas tourists' perceptions of a vernacular tradition. Full-height vertical, white-painted strips mask existing structural elements and, with half-height versions that brace the back panels of the banquette seating, clearly define table spaces within the long narrow plan. Overlapping and intersecting ceiling elements suggest a series of small-scale pitched roofs that relate less precisely to table spaces but visually dominate the black-painted surface of the original roof soffit. These 'roofs' are suspended on wires from the existing structure.

Vertical lattice strips are braced by recessed horizontal members and ceiling strips are held rigid and regular by additional black-painted strips morticed into their back face at 600mm (2 ft) intervals and painted black to make them merge into the existing ceiling plane. Strips cladding existing walls are also painted black. White-painted vertical strips sit in the gaps between the ceiling lengths.

TOP
The central circulation space divides the plan equally. Table spaces are separated by regularly-spaced white-stained timber strips below less regular pitched 'roofs' that hang below the dark 'sky' of the existing roof.

RIGHT
Original diagonal structural members are sandwiched between vertical lattice screens. Black-painted strips connect the clear-stained timbers of the ceiling units.

TOP
Black-stained timbers clad existing solid walls and pass between the inclined ceiling strips, which are continued visually in the vertical recesses and across the seats.

RIGHT
Overlapping, intersecting and off-set lattice elements create more complex secondary patterns.

BOTTOM
1 Entrance
2 Lobby
3 Reception
4 Screen
5 Existing column
6 Table
7 Bench
8 Kitchen

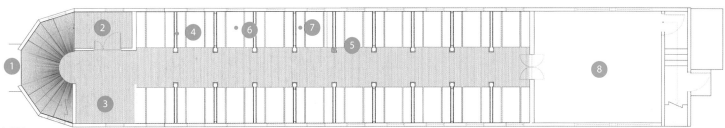

PLAN, SCALE 1:200

THE NAUTILUS PROJECT, SINGAPORE
DESIGN SPIRITS

The entrance to this restaurant, on the fourth floor of a shopping centre, is wide and welcoming. An oyster bar on the left and displays of food on the right lead prospective customers into the main dining area. Curved walls to the service areas are clad in 1mm ($\frac{1}{32}$ in) thick sheets of maple veneer glued to plasterboard. Curved screens to semi-private dining areas are enclosed in 20mm x 15mm ($\frac{13}{16}$ x $\frac{5}{8}$ in) spruce strips fixed at a slope of 20 degrees with a 30mm ($1\frac{3}{16}$ in) gap between them. Both sheets and strips are finished with a 70 percent gloss clear-polyurethane sealer. Both solid and perforated walls share curved windows and door openings and their roughly elliptical forms are echoed in the curved ceiling indents whose backlit sides augment the recessed downlighters in the ceiling.

The external window wall is also lined with screens of spruce strips but these are spaced to give views of the notoriously glamorous Orchard Road below. Maple-veneered ceiling panels and sandblasted Indonesian oak flooring complete the battery of timber finishes. The only exceptions to timber sheet and strip are occasional backlit glass inserts along junctions between solid walls, floor and ceiling, at the edges of openings in the solid walls and the thresholds to semi-private areas.

To assemble the screens is simple, in theory, but difficult to finish to an acceptable level and requires a generous input of skilled labour. The bent spruce strips that make up both faces of the screens are connected, at approximately 15m (5 ft) vertical centres, by wires threaded through their centres and the tensions and counter tensions set up by the bending of the strips give rigidity to the whole. Openings are framed with 2.1mm ($\frac{1}{16}$ in) thick strips of white powder-coated steel and the ends of the spruce strips are pinned, through the steel, using a nail gun. The length of nail that protrudes into the opening is cut and ground smooth. Thin wires threaded vertically through the centres of strips maintain even spacing and improve rigidity.

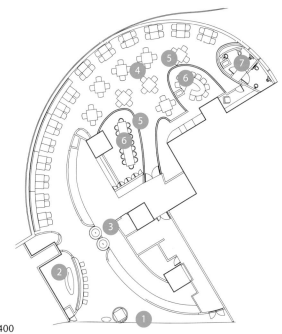

TOP
The skewed curves of the strips that screen private areas and the walls that mask the semi-private areas are echoed in the side-lit ceiling indentations.

MIDDLE
A double skin of plywood strips sets up tensions and counter tensions to stiffen the screen structure. Wires threaded through the middle of each strip maintain regular spacing.

BOTTOM
Plan
1 Entrance
2 Oyster bar
3 Kitchen
4 Dining
5 Lattice screen
6 Semi-private dining
7 WCs

PLAN, SCALE 1:400

TOP
Horizontal strips line the window to the road below. Illuminated glass inserts mark thresholds to semi-private dining areas.

RIGHT
In the bigger semi-private dining area, chairs by Wegener and a raw-edged tabletop continue the commitment to timber. The recessed ceiling light echoes the rectangle of the table rather than the curves of the walls.

FORWARD, BEIJING
SAKO ARCHITECTS

This restaurant, like so many in China, and particularly expensive ones, provides a high percentage of private dining rooms. Extravagant use of floor area ensures that all other tables sit in distinct, clearly defined spaces. The generous planning is complemented by labour-intensive detailing that draws on motifs of traditional Chinese architecture.

From the conventional architecture of the lobby, customers enter the dramatically dark environment of the restaurant through an apparently randomly constructed arch of twigs. Beyond this they can glimpse the hard-edged chrome-and-glass shelving that lines the wall to the office and the back bar. Free-standing cubic plinths occupy some of the generous floor area beyond which are the red-stained lattice screens that enclose the private rooms. Some of these are subdivided by a retractable partition that is housed in a void between small lavatory rooms. These walls, angled in the vertical plane, are curved on plan, less sinuously than the lattice screens but enough to mask the conventional plan forms of the service and communication core of the block. Internal surfaces that abut the core are also curved.

The lattice screens are perhaps the detail that relates most obviously to traditional precedent. Their delicate construction is stabilized by metal anchorings to the structural floor slabs above the suspended plasterboard ceiling and below the tiled floor finish. The interwoven screens enclose the circular four-person tables and the rectangular banquettes that line the window walls. The ends of the strips, where they are cut to allow access, have a protective edging strip to head height but above that are allowed to project as cut.

Private rooms have carpets, with a pattern that echoes the sinuous lines of the partition plan. Floors in circulation and perimeter table areas continue the dark tiles of the entrance space.

TOP
The perimeter banquettes are entered between the screens. The repetitive pattern of the upright surfaces of bench and table and of the window louvres matches the intensity of the screens.

BOTTOM
Retractable partitions between private rooms slide between lavatory pods.

OPPOSITE
An arch of twigs at the entrance contrasts with the hard-edged cubic chrome-and-glass wall beyond.

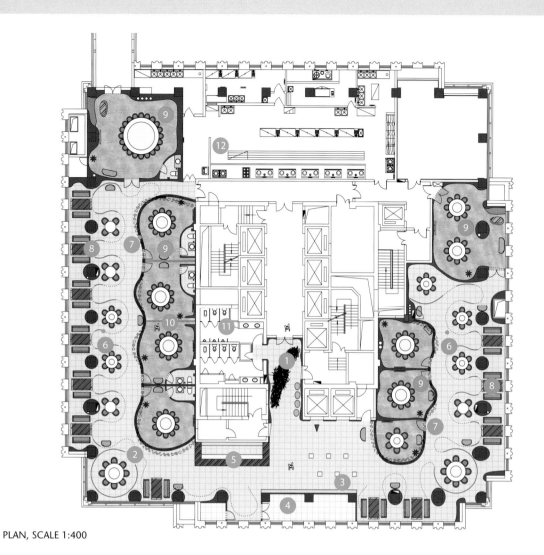

PLAN, SCALE 1:400

BOTTOM LEFT

The red lattice wooden screens and dark wooden panelling contrast with the hard reflective finishes of the bar and entrance area.

BOTTOM MIDDLE

Chrome-and-glass plinths relate to the display walls that line the entrance area.

BOTTOM FAR RIGHT

The circulation zone is bordered by the sinuous inclined dark wooden walls of the private rooms around the service core and the curved lattice screens that allow some views of the existing windows.

TOP LEFT

Detail of screen fixing at ceiling

1 Concrete floor slab
2 Expanding steel anchor
3 6mm (¼ in) steel plate
4 Bolt
5 Timber packing piece
6 Resilient packing material
7 Stained 5mm (³⁄₁₆ in) timber strip
8 Suspended ceiling support grid
9 Painted plaster on 9.5mm (⅜ in) plasterboard
10 Stained 5mm (³⁄₁₆ in) horizontal timber strip
11 Stained 5mm (³⁄₁₆ in) vertical timber strip

TOP RIGHT

Detail of screen fixing at floor

1 Stained 5mm (³⁄₁₆ in) horizontal timber strip
2 Stained 5mm (³⁄₁₆ in) vertical timber strip
3 25mm black granite tile
4 Steel channel
5 Bolt
6 25 x 75mm (1 x 3 in) timber packing piece
7 Screed and levelling screed
8 Concrete sub floor

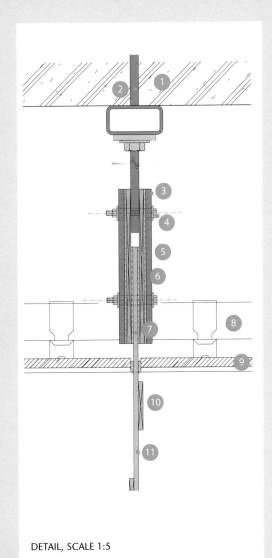

DETAIL, SCALE 1:5

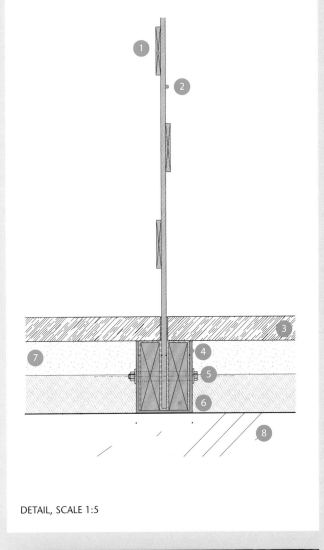

DETAIL, SCALE 1:5

TANG PALACE, HANGZHOU
ATELIER FCJZ

The restaurant is located on the 9m (29½ ft) high sixth and top floor of a superstore in a new area of this rapidly expanding Chinese city. Some of its private rooms, a traditional component of restaurants in China, are suspended from the roof of the original building shell. Detailing makes generous use of bamboo, traditionally in lengths of the natural material and, less familiarly, in the flat strips of reconstituted bamboo used to make up the serpentine wall and interwoven to make the perforated and continuous planes of screens and ceilings.

A staggered bank of banquette seating and tables makes a transition between the rectangular blocks of the reception desk and the freestanding tables in the middle of the floor, but the pervasive bamboo theme is already established in the curved walls of the entrance area and taken up comprehensively in the perforated curved walls that mask the rectilinear walls of the service core and the new kitchen. This serpentine wall gives structure to the central dining spaces and evolves into the undulating mesh of the ceiling, which hangs between the two levels and permits appreciation of the full height of the original shell. Where straight walls, such as those to the kitchen are not softened by a mesh screen, their surfaces are broken by panelled surfaces that are illuminated, on their upper levels.

The real drama of the interior, however, is provided by the private dining rooms, suspended from the existing structure and accessed by suspended walkways. Their circular soffits provide a light source for tables in the central space, which draws attention to their existence. Their circular plans are echoed in the curved screens that begin to enclose five tables in the lower central space. The bigger wholly enclosed and self-contained private rooms use the staggered plan motif of the banquettes, which effectively incorporates their service elements, to make the transition to the curved mesh that surrounds the central space.

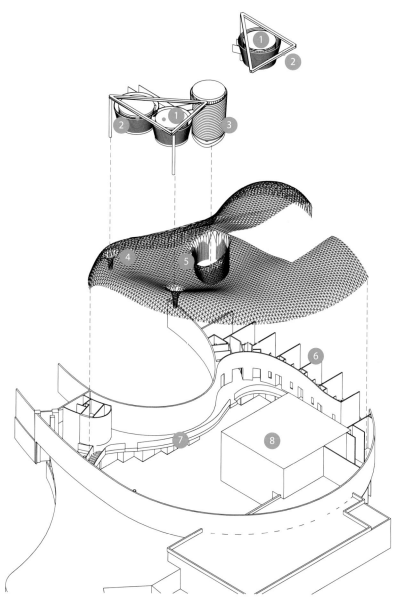

TOP
Lengths of natural bamboo, attached top and bottom to curved timber strips, provide a degree of privacy for the more isolated tables on the lower level.

BOTTOM
1 Suspended private rooms
2 Supporting structure
3 Stacked private rooms
4 Horizontal mesh between floors
5 Void for stacked private rooms
6 Private rooms
7 Glass balustrade
8 Circulation and service core

OPPOSITE TOP
The private rooms, suspended from the original roof structure, provide drama on both upper and lower levels. The glass balustrades to the walkways maximize views of the mesh ceiling.

OPPOSITE BOTTOM
Section
1 Suspended private room
2 Stacked private room
3 Private room
4 Tables

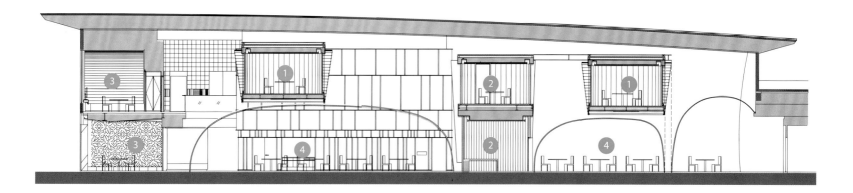

SECTION A-A, SCALE 1:300

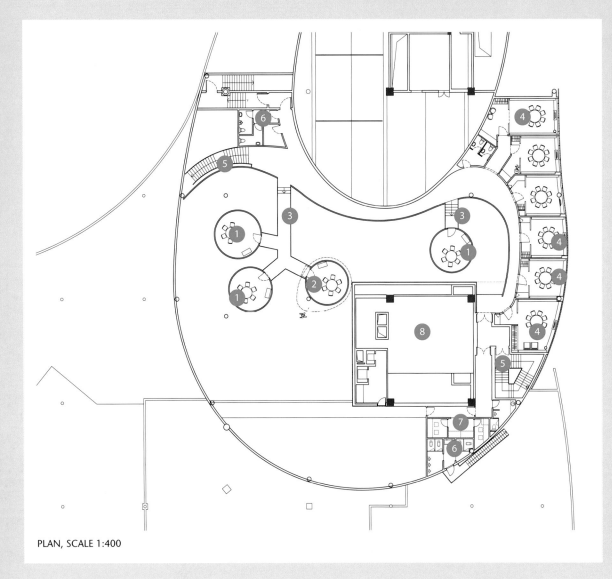

PLAN, SCALE 1:400

LEFT
Plan: upper level
1 Suspended private rooms
2 Private room supported on room below
3 Suspended walkway
4 Private room
5 Stair
6 WCs
7 Office
8 Circulation and service core

BELOW
Plan: lower level
1 Entrance
2 Reception
3 Aquarium
4 Bar
5 Banquettes
6 Tables
7 Private rooms
8 Lattice wall
9 Stair
10 Lightbox
11 Kitchen
12 WCs
13 Circulation and service core

PLAN, SCALE 1:400

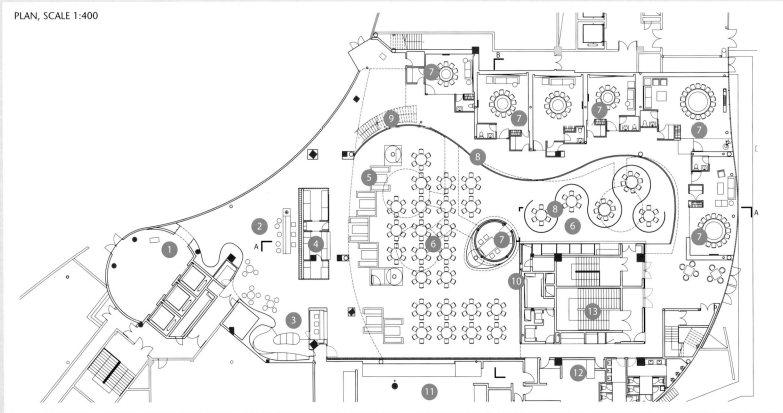

TOP
A mesh of reconstituted bamboo strips makes a perforated ceiling plane between the two levels and provides a smooth transition into the vertical screens that mask existing wall surfaces. The glass-block wall to the bar servery offers a variation on the mesh pattern.

RIGHT
The ceiling mesh allows views of the suspended rooms on the upper level and their illuminated soffits provide the principal light source to the central dining area. The mass of the wall to the stair and service area behind is broken by illuminated panels.

+GREEN, TOKYO
SINATO

This organic restaurant, shop and takeaway is appropriately located close to Komazawa Park, one of the biggest outdoor spaces in the city. The site presents particular challenges. The overall height of the shell is 4.39m (14 ft 4 in), not quite enough to allow the insertion of two levels with conventional floor-to-ceiling heights, and this restriction radically influenced plans and sections. The takeaway and reception is at the street level. Three steps lead up to the shop, which is 0.56m (1 ft 8 in) above entrance level, and nine lead down 1.61m (5 ft 3 in) to the restaurant.

The choice of materials gives coherence to the complex organization. The existing smooth, poured concrete planes of walls, floor and ceiling, together with the service pipes they support, are left exposed. Insertions of rectangular brick boxes, which rise to the level of the shop floor and to knee height in the entrance, create small shared and some more private dining areas at the bottom level. The boxes also contain the kitchen, which is tucked beneath the shop, and are spaces for storage. Brick construction lends itself easily to, and prescribes dimensions for, the perforated pattern making.

A smooth white, steel-framed serpentine wall sits lightly on the brick rectangles, creating a central atrium, the upper part of which has a plan quite different from the lower. It also screens the existing concrete walls but is pierced with variously sized rectangular openings that frame views of the restaurant from the entrance level. The sides of the single, centrally located stair that connects the three levels are clad in horizontal timber strips that match the layering and colour of the brickwork but the quality of detailing and execution of junctions throughout the interior is such that all elements clearly retain their visual autonomy.

TOP LEFT
The entrance level with the takeaway counter on the left, the wooden stair and white curved upper wall behind.

TOP RIGHT
Plan at entrance level
1 Entrance
2 Terrace
3 Takeaway (private room under)
4 Stair
5 Shop (kitchen under)
6 Main restaurant
7 Private room (lower level)
8 Perforated brick wall (lower level)
9 Curved wall
10 Planting boxes
11 Original concrete walls

BOTTOM LEFT
The stair makes minimum contact with floor and wall. Its horizontal layering and colour relate to the brickwork and its curve to the white wall.

BOTTOM RIGHT
A view from the landing at entrance level up to the shop. The brick threshold between takeaway space and stair illustrates how floor levels respond precisely to brick coursing. Translucent glass screens with glued joints in the takeaway and shop contrast with the brick's solidity.

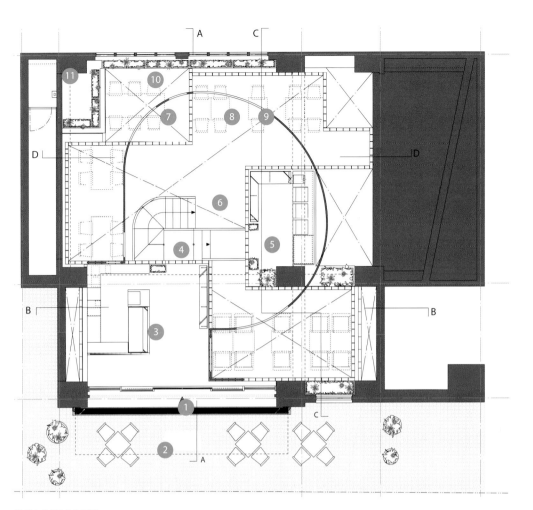

PLAN, SCALE 1:200

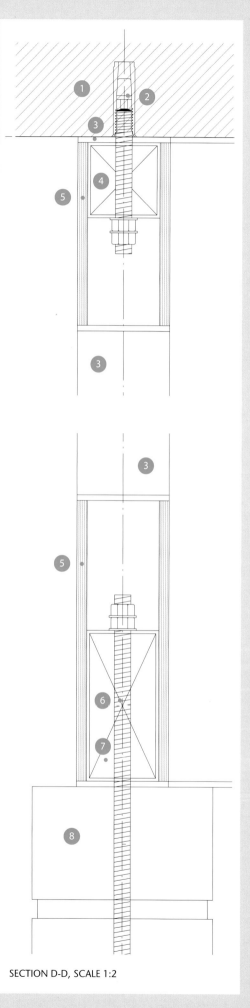

TOP LEFT

Brick coursing determines variations in floor levels, here to a private room. The curved white wall ties private and communal spaces together. The timber strips that clad the walls to the stairs also form treads and risers.

BOTTOM LEFT

The major elements touch but remain visually intact. The white wall rests on but does not intersect the brickwork. Brick dimensions and construction techniques determine perforations in the brick wall.

RIGHT

Section through curved wall
1 Existing concrete slab
2 Steel expansion anchor and 9mm (⅜ in) bolt
3 Curved painted timber board
4 Timber framing
5 Painted fibre-reinforced gypsum board
6 9mm (⅜ in) bolt
7 Timber framing
8 New brick wall

SECTION D-D, SCALE 1:2

TOP RIGHT
Section AA
1 Terrace
2 Takeaway
3 'Window'
4 Curved wall
5 Planting box
6 Private room
7 Stair
8 'Hall'

MIDDLE RIGHT
Section BB
1 Takeaway
2 Curved wall
3 'Window'
4 'Hall'
5 Private room (restricted height)
6 Store

LOWER MIDDLE RIGHT
Section CC
1 Curved wall
2 Shop
3 'Hall'
4 Kitchen
5 Planting box

BOTTOM RIGHT
Section DD
1 Curved wall
2 Shop
3 'Hall'
4 Kitchen
5 Planting box
6 Store

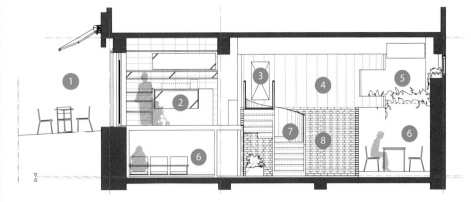

SECTION A-A, SCALE 1:100

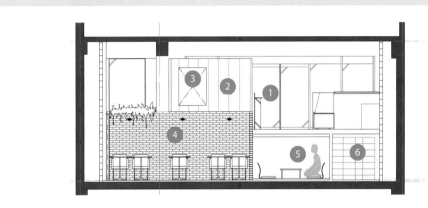

SECTION B-B, SCALE 1:100

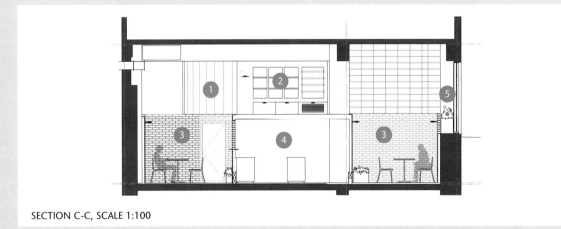

SECTION C-C, SCALE 1:100

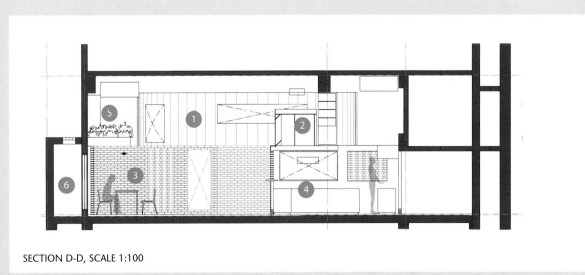

SECTION D-D, SCALE 1:100

MACHO!, STOCKHOLM
GUISE

This is the first of an anticipated chain of Tex-Mex fast-food restaurants and the brief asked that some reference be made to Mexican culture. The designers looked at traditional architectural forms and recognized potential in the Aztecs' stepped pyramid – if it was inverted – and this inspired the form of booths, bar tables and the waiters' station. Only the corner plinth for plants between the front and back areas retains a semblance of the conventional stepped profile.

All the furniture, apart from the chairs, which conform satisfactorily to the predominantly black and white colour scheme, was custom-built for the project, fabricated from welded metal with all seams and corners ground and polished to produce perfectly smooth surfaces for the powder-coated paint finish. The booths in particular are important in this, and future roll-outs, in that they serve to structure the plan, subdividing areas and controlling the flow of customers.

The most deliberate element for guiding customers however is the double row of hot-red, powder-coated, angled metal rods that direct new arrivals to the reception desk and demarcate the public parts of the restaurant from the rear service area. The rods stretch from floor to ceiling and their angles are echoed in the horizontal U-channels suspended from the ceiling and through which hang naked light bulbs, in red holders with red cabling. Angled rods also provide legs for the tables in both the black free-standing booths and the white wall versions in the rear area.

Angles appear again in the fine black lines incised into the walls, which are wholly white apart from images suggestive of Mexico set into occasional triangles. The same angled black lines decorate the speckled white terrazzo floor finish.

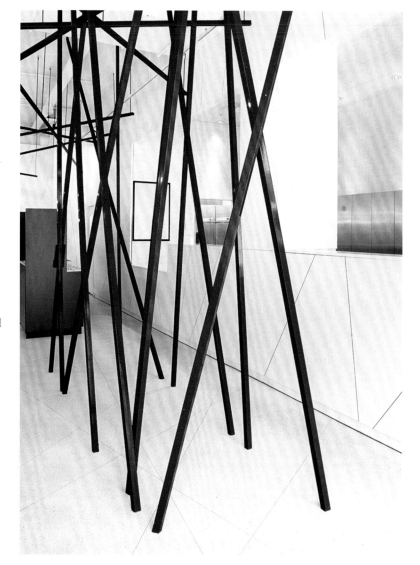

TOP
Angle rods filter new customers to the reception and separate the serving counter from seating.

RIGHT
A wall booth in the rear area.

OPPOSITE
The rear area, looking towards the front. The vertical rods mark the transition to service areas.

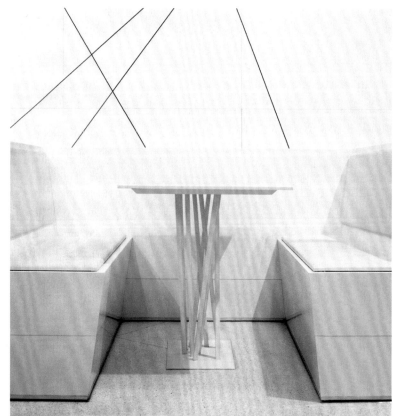

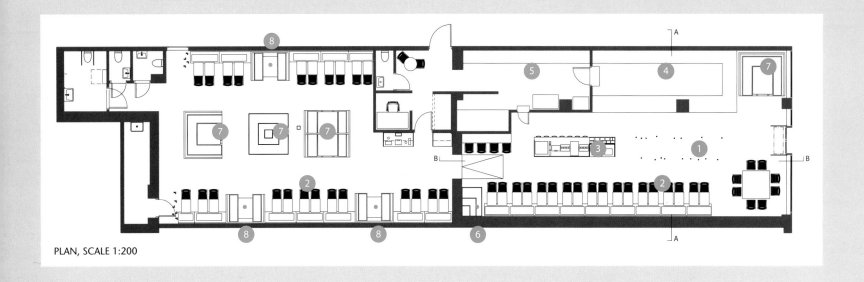

PLAN, SCALE 1:200

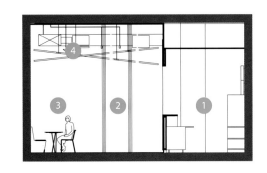

SECTION A-A, SCALE 1:150

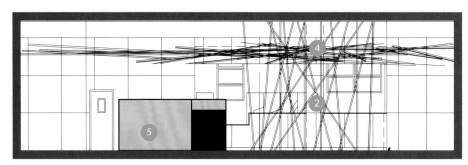

SECTION B-B, SCALE 1:150

ABOVE TOP
Plan
1 Vertical red rods
2 Wall benches/tables/chairs
3 Reception
4 Service counter
5 Kitchen area
6 Cactus plinth
7 Free-standing booths
8 Wall booth

ABOVE MIDDLE
Sections
1 Service counter
2 Vertical red rods
3 Wall benches/tables/chairs
4 Horizontal red rods
5 Reception

LEFT
The wall seating in the front area finishes against the cactus-bearing plinth. The red wall image creates a cactus from chillies.

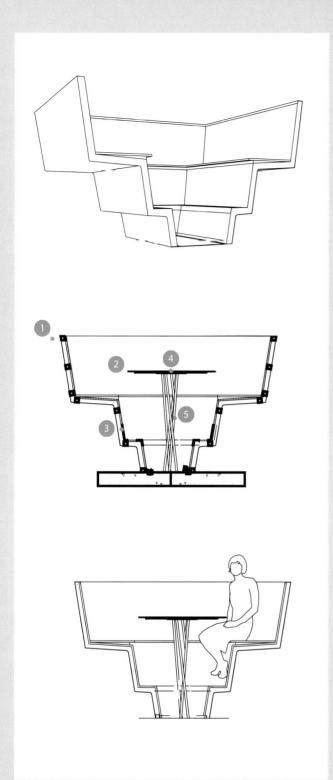

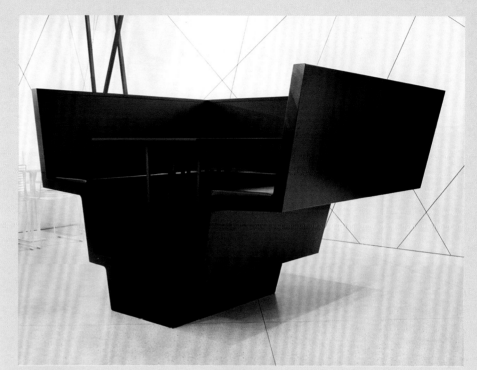

ABOVE

Free-standing booth

1 Welded steel structural skin, ground smooth, powder-coated paint finish

2 Black plastic cushion

3 Foot rest

4 Steel powder-coated tabletop

5 Angles powder-coated steel legs

TOP RIGHT

A free-standing booth in the rear area.

BOTTOM RIGHT

The angled rods meet the floor with precision. The floor joints set up their own angles.

DOGMATIC, NEW YORK
EFGH

This is the flagship restaurant for the Dogmatic Gourmet Sausage System, a company whose name ('dog' being short for hotdog) suggests an ironically proselytizing commitment to their trade; one that deserves a radical interior, well-made with quality ingredients and wit. The solution draws on the robust aesthetics of the butcher's shop, with a 4.3 x 1.2m (14 X 4 ft) butcher's block communal table as its centre-piece, lights hung from ceiling tracks by meat hooks and white faceted wall tiles.

Steel custom-built floor-to-ceiling windows pivot to open the interior to the street but the door proper directs customers into a queuing area in which they are confronted with the 3.3m (10 ft 8 in) tall glass menu board while being held alongside the mural-lined recess that comments facetiously on the process of sausage production and makes rational use of the angled profile of the existing wall.

The opposite wall is lined with a continuous bench, which is cantilevered on steel brackets and divided by narrow shelves for food, drink or elbows. The subdivision is underlined by joints in the blue buttoned, plastic covered backrests through which the cantilevered shelf supports emerge. Top-lit niches in the wall behind contain 'inductees' to the 'sausage hall of fame'. This new wall plane, raised floor and tiled downstand iron out idiosyncrasies in the plan of the original wall.

The communal table dominates the space and the problem of finding chairs to match its bulk without taking up too much circulation space is solved by individual butcher block seating slabs connected to its supporting structure by heavy metal arms that may be slid back under the table. A plate at right angles to the arm projects under the seat to spread the load. The seats are at stool rather than chair height and a foot rest serves standing and sitting customers equally.

RIGHT
The table defines the mural-lined entrance space on the left and the 'wall of fame' with its continuous bench on the right. The edge blocks of the table are elongated to imply even greater bulk.

LEFT
Windows pivot open. The inflated scale of the signage matches that of the communal table.

BOTTOM
Plan
1 Door
2 Pivoting windows
3 Communal table
4 Cantilevered seats
5 Mural-filled recess
6 Menu board
7 Kitchens
8 Continuous bench
9 Cantilevered shelves
10 Plinth
11 'Wall of fame'

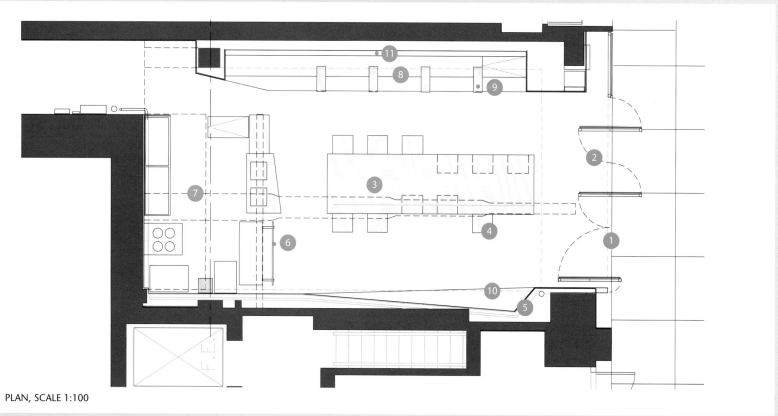

PLAN, SCALE 1:100

TOP

The mural recess makes a virtue of the angle of the original wall.

RIGHT

The tiled downstand and pier make a portal that overrides random elements along the existing wall. Narrow cantilevered tables subdivide the bench. The recesses purport to contain 'inductees' to the 'sausage wall of fame'.

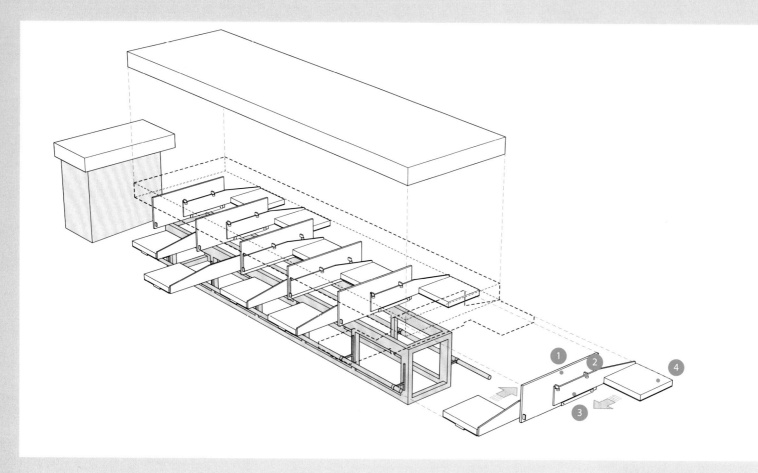

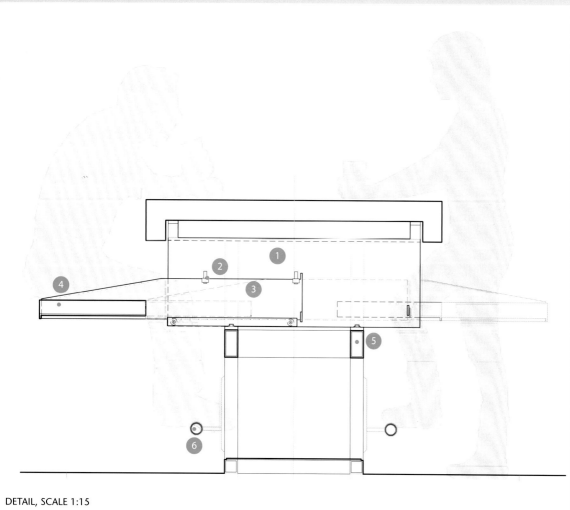

TOP
Table axonometric
1 18mm (¾ in) steel plate fin
2 Ball-bearing cam follower
3 12mm (½ in) steel plate arm
4 50mm (2 in) maple butcher's block seat

LEFT
Table cross section
1 18mm (¾ in) steel plate fin
2 Ball-bearing cam follower
3 12mm (½ in) steel plate arm
4 50mm (2 in) maple butcher's block seat
5 Hollow steel section base frame
6 Steel footrest

DETAIL, SCALE 1:15

TOP
The support arm rolls out on ball bearings and is held back against the table frame by horizontal wheels. The supporting plate for the seat has a lug for finger grip.

RIGHT
The meat hook suspension system is a modest but obvious allusion to the butcher's shop aesthetic.

EL PORTILLO, TERUEL
STONE DESIGNS

The exterior of this log cabin at the Javalambre ski station is painted black so that it contrasts with the snow, like the rocks and trees. Its unglamorous bulk is relieved by the white-painted creatures, by the graphic artist Pepa Prieto, that present a more frivolous public face.

The interior's role is to provide skiers with a place for brief rest and refreshment between runs. It is sparsely furnished, to ease circulation for bulkily clad customers, and painted white, except for the black-painted slot of the servery and the kitchen wall, to maximize the effect of natural light during overcast days.

A red climbing rope, stretched tight, snakes across walls and ceilings, ignoring the conventional geometry of the room. It is reiterated in the bench seating, where it performs as a decorative sleeve for the bent steel legs. Lengths set into grooves cut into the top of the pine seat suggest that the legs are a single continuous element.

The robust tables are also solid pine with their edges painted green, to match that used in the owners' branding. A folded metal strip protects the top of the low-level horizontal timber framing from abuse by ski boots. The white polycarbonate cylinder light fittings that hang above each table are specially produced for the project and loosely draped with lengths of green textile that bring a little more colour to the room. Custom-made coat hooks, carrying the company logo and colour, good humouredly suggest antlers wall-mounted as trophies. The menu is handwritten on masking tape that is stuck to the black wall of the servery, confirming the cafe's informality and allowing easy menu changes.

PLAN, SCALE 1:100

TOP
White graphics break up the black mass and have the visual texture of the trampled snow.

BOTTOM
Plan
1 Entrance
2 Tables and benches
3 Cloth-draped lights
4 Servery counter

OPPOSITE TOP
The stretched red rope ignores the conventional geometry of the room and is used in the sleeve that covers the steel rod bench legs.

OPPOSITE BOTTOM
Sections and plans of benches and tables.

SECTION, SCALE 1:50

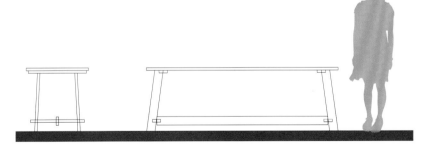

SECTION, SCALE 1:50

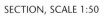

PLAN, SCALE 1:50

PLAN, SCALE 1:50

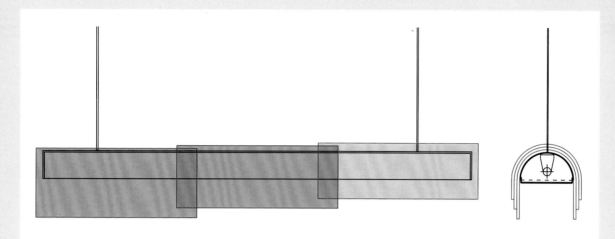

LEFT
Side and end elevations of light fittings.
Longer pieces overlap shorter pieces.

BOTTOM
Green fabric is loosely draped over the
custom-made light fittings. Menu details
are written on masking tape and stuck to
the black wall.

DETAIL, SCALE 1:15

TOP

Edges of table ends are painted corporate green. A metal strip protects the footrest. The red 'rope' appears to be a continuous element, threaded through the pine seat and slotted into a groove.

BOTTOM LEFT

The red sleeve on the metal table legs matches the rope stretched across walls and floor. Coat hangers suggest wall-mounted trophy antlers.

BOTTOM RIGHT

Lengths of green fabric are fixed together with buttons. The red stitching echoes the rope.

KWINT,
BRUSSELS
SAQ

This restaurant is located in a renovated and enclosed arcade. The restored structure was of a quality that deserved exploitation as one of the three significant elements in the new interior. The other two were new, a suspended sculptural form and a padded wall that separates the dining room from the kitchen, service areas and lavatories.

The 30m (10 ft) long copper form, whose colours empathize with those of the brick and stone, also emphasizes the length of the room but lessens its perceived height and provides a suggestion of intimacy for diners. Its glossy metallic finish reflects daylight through the floor-to-ceiling windows and, by night, spotlights positioned around the perimeter of the room level with the bottom of the arches. It begins as a crumpled form that wraps around the bar and performs both as the bar counter and a skin to conceal the practical mechanics. Its complexity suggests something organic that contrasts with the geometric precision of the stone arches and brick vaults. Its comparative lightness allows it to be hung discretely by thin wires, supported on expansion bolts set into the mortar joints of each arch.

The third element, the wall padded with a 90 percent wool fabric, provides a significant absorbent surface to reduce noise within the restaurant, and the heating and ventilating system is concealed behind it. Its buttons, while they refer to a traditional upholstery technique appropriate to a good restaurant, are primarily used to make an irregular pattern that shadows the form of the suspended sculpture. Its visual softness is a counterpoint to the hard surfaces of the other two principal elements and the colour has affinities with the stone of the arches.

TOP LEFT
The crumpled metal form of the bar confronts the entrance before rearing up to run the length of the restaurant at high level. The padded wall conceals the service areas.

TOP RIGHT
The high-level element is suspended by wires set into the joints of the structural arches.

BOTTOM LEFT
The button pattern on the padded wall roughly follows the tracking of the suspended element.

BOTTOM RIGHT
By night, the colours of the new elements blend even more sympathetically with the original brick and stone.

PRAQ,
AMERSFOORT
TJEP

Even children used to eating in conventional restaurants are liable to find themselves alienated from their surroundings after a visit that is too long, or on the wrong day. And even restaurants that set out to cater for families are prone to short change them with arbitrary applications of cartoon characters and, at best, a modest, carefully demarcated playing area. Praq, located within a monumental timber structure, fuses play objects and practical furniture with enough whimsical detail to engage children's imaginations and enough wit to prevent parental alienation. However, for adults who want complete segregation there is a separate room.

The family wing is dominated by a 6m (20 ft) high, scallop-edged screen that divides the larger space, in which tables morph into play structures, from that containing a more conventional collection of large tables. The white paint and geometry of the screen, perforated with circular openings, some infilled with coloured glass, and the diagonal chequerboard floor pattern of square black-and-white tiles contrasts with the brown grain of the timber structure. The purist geometry of circles and squares connects floor tiles and screen apertures and the perforations are reworked in the 'tunnel benches'.

All new elements use colour to set themselves apart from the timber roof structure. Wooden elements are painted and sheet materials are laminated. Coloured glass in the screens lays a film of colour over internal views. The separate adult room makes more restrained use of some of the motifs from the children's zone. White circles on glass make a negative version of the perforated screen. Transparent coloured sheets subdivide the volume and the clear orange glass of the round-ended tabletop, with its overblown legs, retains some of the playful spirit.

TOP
The solid door stabilizes the fragile perforated screen, through which structures and services pass. The empty 'window' on the end of the table protects it from the circulation zone and aligns with the real window on the exterior wall.

RIGHT
The high 'bus' table sits in front of the raised 'movie house' with its cut-out elevations and diagrammatic stairs.

OPPOSITE TOP
Flat planes, geometric patterns and coloured transparencies contrast with the textures of the timber structure.

OPPOSITE BOTTOM
Plan
1 Entrance
2 Bar
3 Kids' and parents' space
4 Adults' space
5 Kitchen
6 Tunnel benches
7 Window table
8 Car table
9 Bus table
10 Movie house
11 Drawing table
12 Kitchen table
13 Game table
14 WCs

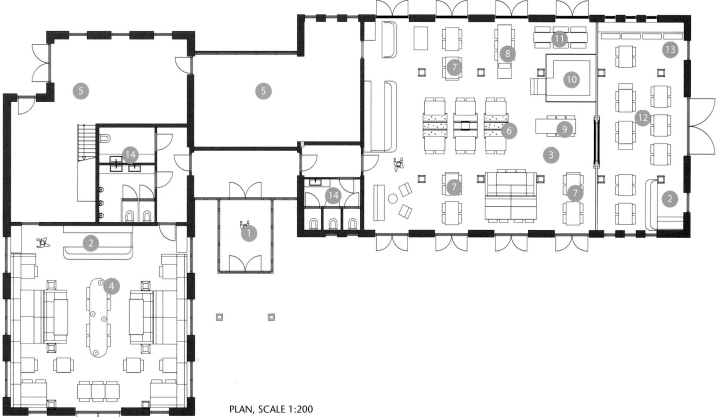

PLAN, SCALE 1:200

OPPOSITE

The adults' area shows more restrained variations on the motifs. White circles on glass are a negative version of the perforated screen.

TOP RIGHT

The transparent red screens fixed to the backs of booths and the overhead beams match those in the children's zone. Round wall lights refer back to the perforated screen. The orange glass tabletop on its inflated, eccentrically distributed legs is a joke for adults.

BOTTOM

A collection of miscellaneous plates are incorporated into the wall lights to provide more adult humour.

SOUS LES CERISIERS, PARIS
RALSTON & BAU

The modest 62sq.m (667 sq.ft) floor area of this Japanese/French fusion restaurant in the centre of Paris is organized to accommodate, in addition to its conventional dining activity, cooking demonstrations by day and a rear area serving a gastronomic menu at night. Prompted by the element of performance implicit in the demonstrations and the elegance of Sakura Franck, the chef, the designers drew on the operatic and geisha traditions of France and Japan respectively to inform their detailing decisions.

Angular, movable panels of 19mm (¾ in) translucent plastic sheet, which provide a degree of privacy between tables, and curved elements of 8mm (⁵⁄₁₆ in) pink opaque plastic sheet suspended from the ceiling subdivide the public area. Both are fixed in position with short lengths of standard metal angle sections, which are hidden beneath the woven vinyl floor covering or located on the side of the ceiling panels away from the entrance and invisible to customers making their first appraisal of the interior. Together, wall and ceiling panels suggest the 'flats' of theatrical scenery. The space is further divided into two colour zones. A bright space, dominated by a counter, which acts as the demonstration kitchen by day and the bar by night, is counterbalanced by the dark finishes of the seating zones. The angle of their intersection sets up a forced perspective, suggesting a deeper plan. The angled planes of the countertop reflect and reconcile the geometries of the existing building shell and the junction of light and dark zones. The bar counter and tabletops are made from a solid core material manufactured from recycled industrial plastic waste and which is itself recyclable. A small 'souffleur' window connects the public area to the kitchen.

Smaller scale details draw on the two nation's cultural references. The logo is derived from the soft curves of a traditional Japanese textile costume clasp and the golden menu cards are pre-punched to allow the insertion of changing menu sheets with classical theatrical costume ribbon, a different one for each card. French theatrical references are seen in the curtain that masks the service rooms and the original opera costumes draped over the backs of the chairs in the rear that upgrade the simple chairs for their gastronomic status in the evening.

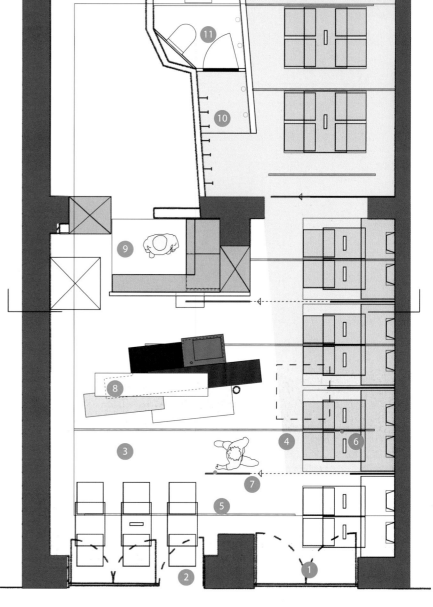

PLAN, SCALE 1:75

TOP
Plan
1 Entrance
2 Window
3 Light-coloured floor
4 Dark floor
5 Ceiling panels
6 Wall panels retracted
7 Wall panels extended
8 Bar/demonstration kitchen
9 Kitchen
10 Cloakroom
11 WCs

BOTTOM
Section

SECTION, SCALE 1:75

TOP
Theatrical costumes dress the chair backs for gastronomic evenings.

RIGHT
Chopstick stands are inspired by costume fixings.

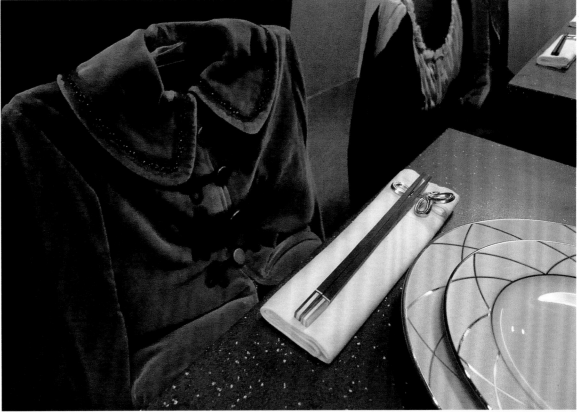

TOP LEFT
The translucencies and shadows of the ceiling and wall panels that articulate the space add complexity. Artificial lighting becomes more intense to the rear.

BOTTOM LEFT
Location and profile of ceiling panels.

BOTTOM RIGHT
Location and profile of wall panels.

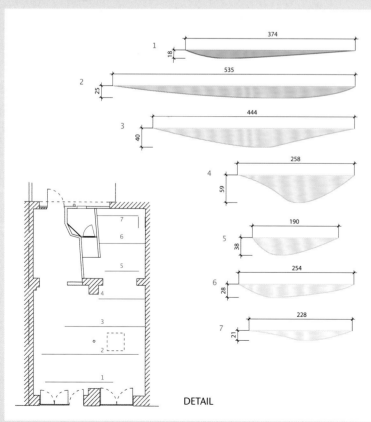

DETAIL

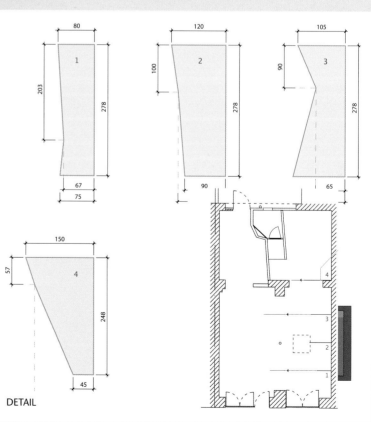

DETAIL

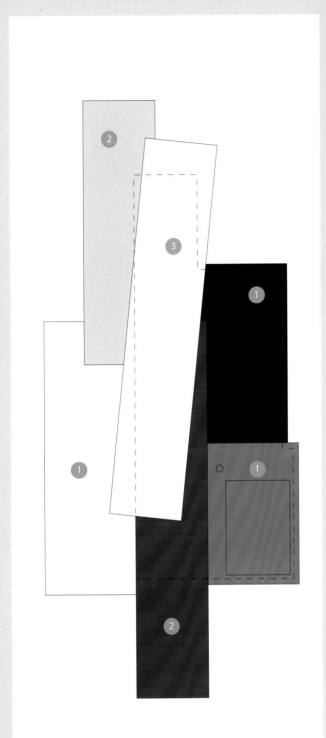

ABOVE LEFT
Plan of bar/demonstration kitchen
1 900mm (35½ in) above floor
2 930mm (36⅝ in) above floor
3 960mm (37¾ in) above floor

TOP RIGHT
Angled planes are determined by the geometries of the floor division and the existing building shell.

BOTTOM RIGHT
The counter, located by the existing column, acts as a demonstration kitchen by day and a bar by night. The small 'souffleur' window gives glimpses of the kitchen.

WHAT HAPPENS WHEN,
NEW YORK
THE METRICS

The idea of the ephemeral 'pop-up' interior is becoming increasingly familiar. It may be applied to the formally commissioned bar or cafe that exists for the duration of a public event, but perhaps it more accurately describes the short-lived commercial experiments that transform unlikely, frequently cheap to rent, locations into places where new commercial propositions are tested and 'hip' brands are launched or relaunched. It always holds the promise of something particular and sits comfortably in the restaurant sector where quality of environment is as important as quality of food.

The idea behind What Happens When might be described as serial pop-up. The building shell is transformed every thirty days, along with the type of food served, the music played and the brand identity, presenting customers with a fresh, and consistently radical, experience. Change becomes the constant. This presents particular problems for the designers, who cannot rely on the qualities of the existing interior to seduce and engage customers. The cost of monthly refits restricts the choice of materials and construction techniques, and installation work needs to be carried out quickly to maximize trading time.

Little is done to the existing shell. Walls, floor and ceiling are painted black, furniture is painted white and remains so throughout all manifestations of the interior. The black planes are relieved by white-painted, oversized versions of the graphic devices and text normally found on construction drawings. Some reproduce typical written notes, those on the ceiling mark lighting power points, those on the floor establish the setting out of tables and chairs. Closely spaced ceiling hooks make a flexible grid of hanging points that encourage different treatments of the ceiling and allow easy relocation of light sources. One of the virtues of the necessarily frugal solutions is that components are readily recognizable so that customers can appreciate the ingenuity of their re-deployments. The making processes used are transparently simple and raise no expectations of undue refinement. The success of the interior depends on wit, which is enough to fuel customers' appetites for return visits.

TOP
A complex matrix of painted, square-sectioned timber strips are suspended from the ceiling hooks. The positions of tables and chairs are painted on the floor using the conventions of plan drawing.

BOTTOM
Familiar objects, like the rough wooden nesting box, transformed by pink paint, confirm the interior's intention to amuse and divert.

TOP
Hanging fabric swatches in gradated hues and tones shift attention to the ceiling and moderate the acoustics.

RIGHT
Ceiling hooks create a regular grid but each loosely hanging fabric swatch assumes a distinctive shape. The graphic symbol for a power source is visible behind the aggregated light bulbs.

LEFT
Lengths of cloth draped loosely over poles, skewed on plan, hanging from the ceiling hooks and fixed to the walls, change the geometry of the room. Spherical light bulbs hang through gaps in the fabric.

BOTTOM LEFT
Undraped wall and ceiling areas are ironically enhanced by cantilevered shelves of backlit, white-painted objets d'art and 'chandeliers' that are assemblages of standard bulb holders. Table settings reinforce the genteel references.

BELOW
A 'chandelier' light fitting.

BOTTOM RIGHT
White-painted 'objets d'art'.

TOP LEFT
Assorted tassels shade a naked bulb in the lavatory. The tiles are painted white.

BOTTOM LEFT
Lengths of roughly cut white-painted timber strips are glued to a horizontal sheet hung from the ceiling hooks.

TOP RIGHT
Cords threaded between hooks on walls and ceiling make a mesh of varying densities. Wall-, ceiling- and floor-mounted light fittings are assembled from painted lengths of timber and circles of composite board.

MIDDLE RIGHT
Circles, of diameter slightly less than the spherical light bulbs, are cut into the thin metal sheet and perform as reflectors and are adjustable for angle and direction.

BOTTOM RIGHT
Each tile in the lavatories is decorated with miniaturized versions of the coloured circles used in the light fittings.

RESOURCES

AUSTRALIA

Koichi Takada Architects Pty Ltd
Suite 5.1 (Level 5)
2 Hill Street, Surrey Hills
NSW 2010, Australia
info@koichitakada.com
www.koichitakada.com
Cave; Tree

BELGIUM

SAQ Brussels
Arenbergstraat 44
1000 Brussels
Belgium
T: +32 23 005 910
info@saq.eu
www.saq.eu
Kwint; Die Kunstbar

CHINA

3Gatti
Office K, Floor 2
169 Jinxian Road
200020 Shanghai
China
shanghai@3gatti.com
www.3gatti.com
T: +86 21 6208 2226
F: +86 21 6208 2226
Zebar

Atelier Feichang Jianzhu
Yuan Ming Yuan East Gate,
Northside, Yard No.1
Hai Dian District
100084 Beijing
China
T: +86 10 8262 6123
F: +86 10 8262 2712
fcjz@fcjz.com
www.fcjz.com
Tang Palace

FRANCE

Matali Crasset Productions
26 Rue du Buisson
Saint Louis
F-75010 Paris, France
matali.crasset@wanadoo.fr
www.matalicrasset.com
La Ménagerie De Verre

Studio Robert Stadler
8 Rue Saint-Marc
75002 Paris
France
T: +331 4874 5981
info@robertstadler.net
www.robertstadler.net
Corso Café

GERMANY

designliga
Bureau for Visual Communication
and Interior design
Hans-Preissinger-Strasse 8
Halle A
81379 Munich
Germany
T: +49 89 624 219 47
hello@designliga.com
www.designliga.com
Das Neue Kubitscheck

TULP Design Gmbh
Gotzinger Strasse 52b
81371 Munich
Germany
info@tulp.de
www.tulp.de
Yellow Submarine

INDIA

Mancini Enterprises Pvt. Ltd.
17 Crescent Avenue
Kesavaperumalpuram
Chennai 600028
India
T: +91 44 24614000
F: +91 44 24617047
architects@mancini-design.com
www.mancini-design.com
Mocha Mojo

Serie Architects Mumbai
317 A-Z Industrial Estate
G.K. Road, Lower Parel
Mumbai 400013
India
Blue Frog

ITALY

Francesco Moncada
VialeTica 85
96100 Siracuse
Italy
T: +39 338 3007953
mail@francescomoncada.com
www.francescomoncada.com
Pizza Perez

JAPAN

Design Spirits Co., ltd
Tokyo office
2-18-2-202 Oh-hara Setagaya-ku
Tokyo
156-0041 Japan
T: +81 3 3324 9901
info@design-spirits.com
www.design-spirits.com
Beijing Noodle No. 9; Niseko Lookout Café; The Nautilus Project

Himematsu Architecture
402 Sanko
1-18-3 Higashi Shibuya-Ku
Tokyo
Japan 150-0011
T: +81 3 34860308
info@himematsu.jp
www.himematsu.jp
Vinegar Café

Kidosaki Architects Studio
1-5-12, Ginza
Chuo-ku
Tokyo
104-0061 Japan
T: +81 3 3562 2235
info@kidosaki.com
www.kidosaki.com
AG Café

Sako Architects
Tokyo office
3-2-12 Nihonbashihoncho
Chuou-ku
Tokyo
Japan
Forward

Sinato
3-12-5-101 Tsurumaki
Setagaya-ku

Tokyo 154-0016
Japan
T: +81 3 6413 9081
F: +81 3 6413 9082
central@sinato.jp
www.sinato.jp
Salon Des Saluts; +green

LEBANNON

Paul Kalustian
31 Industrial City
Leon Bros Building – GF
Dekwane, Beirut
Lebannon
T: +961 1 490453
info@paulkalustian.com
www.paulkaloustian.com
MYU

THE NETHERLANDS

Puresang
Frankrijklei 125
2000 Antwerpen
The Netherlands
T: +32 474 69 04 02
info@pure-sang.com
www.pure-sang.com
Grey Goose Bar

Studio Makkink & Bey
Postbus 909
3000 AX Rotterdam
The Netherlands
press@jurgenbey.nl
www.studiomakkinkbey.nl
KaDE

Tjep
Veembroederhof 204
1019 HC Amsterdam
The Netherlands
goodnews@tjep.com
www.tjep.com
Praq; Pluk

NORWAY

Ralston & Bau
Transplant
N-6963 Dale I Sunnifjord
Norway
www.ralstonbau.com
T: +47 5773 5200
Sous Les Cerisiers

POLAND

Grupa xm3
grupa.xm3@gmail.com
www.xm3.com.pl
T: 694 396 326
Zmianatematu

Wunderteam.pl
Ul. Wierzbowa 24/26/19
90-245 Lodz
Poland
info@wunderteam.pl
www.wunderteam.pl
MS Café

SLOVENIA

Elastik
Poljanska cesta 06
SI-1000 Ljubljana
Slovenia
info@elastik.net
www.elastik.net
Thai Restaurant

SPAIN

Barbara Appolloni Architect
Carrer Lledó 5
1o 3a
Barcelona 08002
Spain
T: +34 645816268
contact@barbaraappolloni.com
www.barbaraappolloni.com
Federal Café

**MSB Estudi-taller d'arquitectura
i disseny**
C/St. Grau 13-46
17855 Montagut
Girona
Spain
T: +34 675255421
msbestuditaller@gmail.com
www.msbestuditaller.com
6T7 Espai Café

Stone Designs
C/ Segovia 10. 28005.
Madrid
Spain
T: +34 91 540 03 36
info@stone-dsgns.com
www.stone-dsgns.es
El Portillo

SWEDEN

Guise
Katarina Vastra Kyrkogata 8
116 25 Stockholm
Sweden
info@guise.se
www.guise.se
Macho!

**Jonas Wagell Design &
Architecture**
Lindvallspan 10, ground floor
SE-117 36 Stockholm
Sweden
info@jonaswagell.se
www.jonaswagell.se
Design Bar 2010

Note Design Studio
Heliosgatan 13
120 30 Stockholm
Sweden
T: +46 8 656 88 04
info@notedesignstudio.se
www.notedesign studio.se
Café Foam

Studio Greiling
Kallforsvagen 20
124 32 Bandhagen
Sweden
info@katringreiling.com
www.katringreiling.com
Design Bar 2011

SWITZERLAND

aekae llc.
Talweisenstrasse 17
8045 Zurich
Switzerland
mail@aekae.com
www.aekae.com
Z am Park

HHF architects eht sia bsa
Allschwilerstrasse 71A
CH-4055 Basel
Switzerland
T: +41 61 756 70 10
F: +41 61 756 70 11
info@hhf.ch
www.hhf.ch

**Confiserie Bachmann
UK**

Ben Kelly Design
10 Stoney Street
London SE1 9AD
United Kingdom
T: +44 20 7378 8116
info@bkduk.co.uk
www.benkellydesign.com
Factory 251

Outline Projects
10 Stoney Street
Waterloo
London SE1 9AD
United Kingdom
T: +44 20 7378 1616
info@outline-projects.co.uk
www.outline-projects.co.uk
**Bangalore Express Waterloo;
Bangalore Express City**

VONSUNG
51 Carillon Court
London E1 5EN
United Kingdom
T: + 44 207 650 8909
info@vonsung.com
www.vonsung.com
Polka Gelato

USA

EFGH
34 W27th Street, 9th floor
New York
NY 10001
USA
info@efgh-ny.com
www.efgh-ny.com
Dogmatic

Elle Kunnos de Voss
The Metrics
195 Chrystie Street 600A
New York
NY 10002
info@metricsdesigngroup.com
www.metricsdesigngroup.com
What Happens When

Scalar Architecture
PC Interdisciplinary Design
The Scalar Warehouse
195 Chrystie Suite 600E
New York, NY 10002

USA
T: 646 342 2244
F: 212 2602247
info@scalararchitecture.com
www.scalararchitecture.com
Recess

**Stanley Saitowitz/Natoma
Architects Inc.**
(Principal: Stanley Saitowitz,
Associate: Alan Tse)
1022 Natoma Street no.3
San Francisco
CA 94103, USA
info@saitowitz.com
www.saitowtz.com
Conduit; Toast

CREDITS

All architectural drawings are supplied courtesy of the architects. In all cases every effort has been made to credit the copyright holders, but should there be any omissions or errors the publisher will be pleased to insert the appropriate acknowledgment in any subsequent editions of the book.

AG Café Photography: Junji Kojima

Bangalore Express Waterloo/City Client: Waterloo Leisure; Photography: Philip Vile

Beijing Noodle No.9 Commissioned by: Caesar's Palace; Designer: Yuhkichi Kawai Photographer: Barry Johnson

Blue Frog Design: Chris Lee and Kapil Gupta; Photography: Fram Petit

Café Foam Designers: Jon Eliason and Johannes Carlstrom; Design team: Anna Roos, Cristiano Pigazzini, Matthias Sarnholm; Commissioned by Michael Toutonai

La Cantine de la Ménagerie De Verre Photographs courtesy La Ménagerie De Verre; p158 (bottom) pouffe originally designed for HI hotel in Nice, manufactured by Domodinamica; p159 (bottom) Instant chair and Instant table manufactured by Moustache

Cave Design team: Koichi Takada, Sun Mi Kang, Marcellino Sain, Camille Lincoln, Lukas Mersch; Construction team: Darrell Sadler/Finn Projects; Building Regulations Consultants: BCA Logic; Authorities: Sutherland Shire Council; Photography: Sharrin Rees; Construction photographs: Koichi Takada Architects

Conduit Photography: Rien van Rijthoven

Confiserie Bachmann Design team: Herlach Hartmann Frommenwiler with Markus Leixner; Commissioned by: Confiserie Bachmann AG; Photography: Tom Bisig

Corso Café Courtesy: Robert Stadler; Commissioned by Maison Thierry Costes; Photographers: Marc Domage (finished project); Studio RS (work in progress)

Design Bar 2010 Photography: Jonas Wagell Design & Architecture

Design Bar 2011 Designer: Katrin Greiling; Commissioned by Stockholm Furniture Fair; Event coordinator: Johanna Nilsson/Milou Quist; Photographer: Katrin Greiling

Dogmatic Architects: Hayley Eber and Frank Gesualdi; Steel fabrication: The Orchard Group; Photography: Kelly Shimoda

6T7 Espai Café Designer: Miquel Subiras; Photography: Miquel Merce Arquitect

El Portillo Design team: Eva Prego + Cutu Mazuelos; Graphic artist: Pepa Prieto; Photography: Stone Designs

Factory 251 Photography: Kevin Cummins

Federal Café Photography: Lucia Carretero

Forward Design team: Keiichiro Sako, Shihei Aoyama, Yuichiro Imafuku, Ken-ichi Kurimoto; Lighting: Masahide Kakudate Lighting Architect and Associates (Masahide Kakudate, Junichiro Nozawa); Photography: Misae Hiromatsu

+green Designer: Chikara Ohno; Photography: Toshiyuki Yano

Grey Goose Bar Photographs courtesy Puresang

KaDE Photography: Makkink & Bey

Kwint/Die Kunstbar Photographs courtesy SAQ Brussels

Macho! Concept and design: Jani Kristoffersen and Andreas Ferm; Furniture production: Guise Projekt AB; Photography: Jesper Lindstrom

Mocha Mojo Design team: Niels Schoenfelder, Bharath ram, V.S Aneesh, R.Velu, Sangeetha Patrick, Natasha Jeyasingh; Photography: Mancini Enterprises

MS Café Designers: Magdalena Koziej, Paulina Stepien; Graphic design: Hakobo, Jacub Stepien; Photography: Olo Rutkowski, Ula Tarasiewicz

MYU Commissioned by Joe Mourani; Design: Paul Kalustain; Photographer: Joe Keserwani

The Nautilus Project Commissioned by: AC2 Internatinal Pte. Ltd.; Designer: Yuhkichi Kawai; Construction: KNK Construction Pte. Ltd., Edwin Fong; Lighting design: muse-D Inc., Kazuhiko Suzuki; Graphic design: Molotov Creative Pte. Ltd., Alastair Christie; Photographer: Toshide Kajiwara

Das Neue Kubitscheck Photography: Pascal Gambarte

Niseko Lookout Café Commissioned by: YTL Hotels; Designer: Yuhkichi Kawai; Construction: Nomara Co. Ltd.; Lighting design: muse-D Inc., Kazuhiko Suzuki and Misuzu Yagi; Photographer: Toshide Kajiwara

Pizza Perez Design team: Francesco Moncada, Marco Pizzo, Gianluca Conigliaro; Graphics: Marianna Rentzou, Konstantinos Pantazis; Photography: Alberto Moncada

Pluk Design team: Frank Tjepkema, Janneke Hooysmans, Tina Stieger, Leonie Janssen, Bertrand Gravier, Camille Cortet;

Polka Gelato Creative director: Joseph Sung; Branding designer: Michiko Ito; Photography: Joseph Sung and Teresa Wong

Praq Design team: Frank Tjepkema, Janneke Hooysmans, Tina Stieger, Leonie Janssen, Bertrand Gravier, Camille Cortet;

Recess Design Team: Julio Salcedo (Principal) with Elizabeth MacWillie (Associate), Monica Torres (Project Architect), Tholmas Dalmas, Ana Koleva; Lighting design: Attila Uysal Contractor: SCK Teamwork; Photography: Kris Tamburello

Salon Des Saluts Design team: Chikara Ohno with Masaki Ito; Contractor: ZYCC Corporation; Photography: Toshiyuki Yano

Sous Les Cerisiers Photography: Vincent Baillais

Tang Palace Commissioned by: Hong Kong Tang Palace Food & Beverage Group Company Ltd.; Principal designer: Chang Yung Ho; Project architect: Lin Yihsuan; Design team: Yu Yie, Wu Xia, Suiming Wang; Contractor: Shenzhen C.S.C. Decoration Design Engineering Company Ltd; Photography: Shu He

Thai Restaurant Design team: Mika Cimolini, Igor Kebel, Primoz Spacapan; Structural Engineers: Gregor Gruden, Tomo Oblak; Mechanical Engineer: Ziga Lebar; Electrical Engineer: Rafael Lebar; Photography: Vsebina

Toast Photography: Rien van Rijthoven

Tree Design team: Koichi Takada, Robert Chen; Construction team: Bonar Interiors Building Regulations Consultants: BCA Logic; Authorities: Randwick City Council Photography: Sharrin Rees; Construction photographs: Koichi Takada Architects

Vinegar Café Design: Shinichiro Himematsu; Lighting design: ENDO; Contractor: TOH Construction; Copyright: Shinichiro Himematsu

What Happens When Concept: John Fraser; Branding: Emilie Baltz; Composers: Micah Silver (Nordic); Joshua Benyard (Where The Wild Things Are); Renoir (Ball Of Fire Shooting Flame); Diallo Riddle (Jazz); Photography: Felix de Voss

Yellow Submarine Contractor: Schreinerei und Wohnstudio Graf; Photography: Oliver Jung

Z am Park Design: Fabrice Aeberhard and Christian Kaegi; Photography: Nico Scharer

Zebar Chief Architect: Francesco Gatti; Project Manager: Summer Nie; Collaborators: Nicole Ni,Chen Quiju, Kelly Han, Chen Han Yi, Lu Cheng Yuan, Jessie Zhengxin, Ronghui Chen, Vivian Husiyue, Aurgho Jyoti; Photography: Daniele Mattioli

Zmianatematu Design team: Mateusz Wojcicki, Maciej Kurkowski, Julian Nieciecki; Photography: Paulina Sasinowska

ABOUT THE CD

The attached CD can be read on both Windows and Macintosh computers. All the material on the CD is copyright protected and is for private use only.

The CD includes files for all of the drawings included in the book. The drawings for each building are contained in a folder labelled with the project name. They are supplied in two versions: the files with the suffix '. eps' are 'vector' Illustrator EPS files but can be opened using other graphics programs such as Photoshop; all the files with the suffix '.dwg' are generic CAD format files and can be opened in a variety of CAD programs.

Each image file is numbered according to its original location within the book and within a project, reading from left to right and top to bottom of the page, followed by the scale. Hence, '01_01_200.eps' would be the eps version of the first drawing of the first project in the book and has a scale of 1:200.

The generic '.dwg' file format does not support 'solid fill' utilized by many architectural CAD programs. All the information is embedded within the file and can be reinstated within supporting CAD programs. Select the polygon required and change the 'Attributes' to 'Solid', and the colour information should be automatically retrieved. To reinstate the 'Walls'; select all objects within the 'Walls' layer/class and amend their 'Attributes' to 'Solid'.